"Jason Boyett's latest is a long-overdue primer for the thinking man's survivalist. In an age when televangelists are preaching 'pie-in-the-sky-by-and-by,' Jason gives us practical, down-to-earth suggestions on how to handle the messier side of The End of the World with style and sense of humor intact. Think of it as *Chicken Soup for the Damned Soul*. No right-thinking citizen ought be without his/her own copy of *Pocket Guide to the Apocalypse*. Don't leave your home planet without it."

—ROBERT DARDEN, Senior Editor,
THE WITTENBURG DOOR

"This is the full-on bathroom book of the century."

—KATIE MEIER, author,
A GIRL'S GUIDE TO LIFE (NELSON)

POCKET GUIDE
-TO THE-
APOCALYPSE

THE
OFFICIAL
FIELD MANUAL FOR THE
END OF THE WORLD

JASON BOYETT

[RELEVANTBOOKS]
WWW.RELEVANTBOOKS.COM

Published by Relevant Books
A division of Relevant Media Group, Inc.
www.relevantbooks.com
www.relevantmediagroup.com

Design: Relevant Solutions
www.relevant-solutions.com
Cover design by Mark Arnold
Interior design by Jeremy Kennedy

For information or bulk orders:
RELEVANT MEDIA GROUP, INC.
100 SOUTH LAKE DESTINY DR., STE 200
ORLANDO, FL 32810
407-660-1411

For booking information, visit *www.jasonboyett.com*.

International Standard Book Number: 0-9760357-1-5

05 04 03 02 01 10 9 8 7 6 5 4 3 2

Printed in the United States of America

CONTENTS

VII

INTRODUCTION
BEGINNING OF THE END

01

CHAPTER ONE
APOCALYPTIONARY
(A Glossary of the End)

27

CHAPTER TWO
THE END IS NEAR, PART 1
(A Timeline: 2000 B.C. until 1900)

45

CHAPTER THREE
THE END IS NEAR, PART 2
(Another Timeline: 1900 to the Present)

75

CHAPTER FOUR
KNOW YOUR POTENTIAL ANTICHRISTS
(A Gallery of Candidates)

109

CHAPTER 5
FUN WITH ESCHATOLOGY
(A Painless Introduction to Apocalyptic Theory)

129

CHAPTER 6
ARMAGEDDON GRAB-BAG
(Miscellaneous Items Not Long Enough for Chapters of Their Own)

BEGINNING OF THE END

The End is near.

Not to get all Chicken Little on you, but global catastrophe is pretty much inevitable. Could be an act of God. Could be a collision with an asteroid. Nuclear holocaust is a familiar candidate, as is global warming. And even if those options fall through, we're still looking at the spectacular flameout of our sun when it runs out of fuel in five billion years—give or take—at which point it will start swelling up like a flaming cosmic beach ball until it swallows the earth in a spectacular blaze of cataclysmic glory.

So you'd better start getting ready, kids, because the end of the world as we know it could happen this week. It could happen today. It could happen before you even finish this senten—

Still here? Whew. Good thing you're reading this book.

People are more fascinated with apocalyptic prophecy than ever before. This may be due to the dire events happening around the world on a daily basis, especially in the Middle East. But, more likely, this fascination owes itself to the kajillions who have been waiting with sweaty, trembling hands for each new installment of *Left Behind*. Which, for those of you living in caves, is the best-selling series of apocalyptic novels by Tim LaHaye and Jerry Jenkins. They detail the Rapture (the insta-snatching of faithful Christians into heaven), the ascension of the Antichrist, and the glorious Second Coming of Jesus. Good stuff. End-Times publishing hasn't been this hot since Hal Lindsey sold 35 million copies of *The Late, Great Planet Earth* back in the early 1970s.

Want numbers? A Barna Research Group survey in 2001 found that 40 percent of Americans believe the world will end someday thanks to some sort of "supernatural intervention." An Associated Press survey released in 1997 revealed that a quarter of American adults expect this "intervention" to involve the return of Christ—and figure they'll still be around when he shows up. A 2001 *Newsweek* poll found that 52 percent expected Jesus to come back at some point during the next millennium (between the years 2001 and 3000). And four out of five of those familiar with the Left Behind books said it was possible that the fictional events they describe could happen in real life.

Which is probably why, despite a historical success rate over the past two thousand years of, um, *exactly zero*, theologians and preachers and delusional cultists still insist on making end-of-the-world predictions. And why biblical prophecy seminars are all the rage among conservative Christian churches in the South. And why we continue to see the coming Apocalypse in everything from

Y2K to WMD to implantable microchip identification devices (Mark of the Beast alert!). And why everyone—besides Tim LaHaye, of course—is still struggling to understand what the book of Revelation is talking about with all of its horsemen and trumpets and seals and multi-eyed, dragon-headed creatures.

Thank heaven you've got your own sweaty, trembling hands wrapped around *The Pocket Guide to the Apocalypse*. Consider it your personal tour director for the swan song of Old Blue. A jargon decoder. A history professor. An Antichrist identifier. At the least, it may provide some entertaining reading during that blasted Tribulation.

Which is probably right around the corner. Don't get too comfortable.

APOCALYPTIONARY
(A Glossary of the End)

As with any professional specialty, religious system, or hobby—and for Americans, the Apocalypse is all of those things crammed into the same burrito—there's a frustrating "inside baseball" quality to any End-Times discussion. You've got a bunch of terms you may have heard before but don't really understand. Some multisyllabic theological concepts that sound so esoteric they'd baffle even *Left Behind* fanatics. Then there's that perfect volume of clarity, the book of Revelation. Yep, the end of the world has a lingo all its own.

Which is why being stuck with some guy who's convinced the planet is just one or two fulfilled prophecies away from doom can be annoying. Mostly because he's so passionate, he's practically spitting. But also because you have no idea what he's yapping about. Seven Seals? Premillennial dispensationalism? What? It's not too different from being cornered by a near-sighted model train enthusiast who's prattling on about his N-Scale Bachman Spectrum Doodlebug and the elaborate environment he's constructed for it to chug through. Only in this case, the teensy village with its wee bridges and sawmills and midget-bonsai fir trees is going to be annihilated by the fiery wrath of God.

And seeing how that's the subject of this book and everything, this is probably a good time for a crash course on apocalyptic geekspeak. So park your Doodlebug and enjoy.

ABADDON

A chief fallen angel and/or demon of Satan who ascends from the bottomless pit to wreak mayhem, according to Revelation 9:11. He's more than just your average chief fallen angel, though. This dude's the King of the **Locusts**, which are deadly assassins loosed during the fifth **trumpet blast** for the purpose of torturing non-believers. Also known by the Greek name Apollyon, Abaddon is Hebrew for "destroyer," and such names aren't given lightly. Very horrifying.

NOT TO BE CONFUSED WITH: The German death-metal band of the same name, renowned for their combination of classical music with melodic black metal and philosophical lyrics. Also horrifying, but in a completely different way.

PLEASE USE IT IN A SENTENCE: Don't select that mangy dog from the pound. It might be Abaddon.

AMILLENNIALISM

The theological belief that there will not be a literal thousand-year earthly reign, or **millennium**, as described in Revelation 20. Instead, amillennialists interpret the "thousand years" more along the lines of "a really super-long time." They explain that we're already sailing along through the millennium—that the kingdom of God is now present in this world, through the institution of the Church and in the hearts of believers—and all the End-Times events in the Bible either have already taken place or are figurative. Up until the nineteenth century, this was the prevailing belief of most Christians. (*See chapter 5 for a more in-depth discussion of amillennialism.*)

PLEASE USE IT IN A SENTENCE: Amillennialism, as a theory, was first introduced by Saint Augustine. Though, back then, he was just known as "Augustine."

ANTICHRIST

A false messiah and the primary tool of Old Scratch on earth during the Last Days. Usually predicted to be a final world ruler who deceives the masses by promising such yummies as international peace and a one-world government. He gets his followers good and seduced with a number of impressive tricks. These include (but are not limited to) performing fraudulent miracles, controlling the world's economy, and break-dancing. (Maybe not that last one.) The Antichrist is akin to a devious evil twin of Jesus, in that his hidden agenda is not just the world domination thing but also to oppose Christianity by torturing and destroying all those who refuse to lick his proverbial boots. But not for long, as Jesus also has an agenda—to expose the Antichrist as a fraud, go medieval on his pointy satanic tail during the battle of **Armageddon**, and reign for a thousand years in his stead. According to **dispensationalist** theology, the Antichrist is scheduled to appear halfway through the **Tribulation**. There will be a parade.

Many people throughout history have been pegged as the Antichrist, including the Roman Emperor Nero, Adolf Hitler, John F. Kennedy, Mikhail Gorbachev, Ronald Reagan, and Bill Gates. (*See chapter 4 for more than you ever wanted to know about candidates for the Antichrist.*) Being named a potential Antichrist is kind of an honor, if you can look past the whole "personification of evil" thing.

PLEASE USE IT IN A SENTENCE: I blame the frequent crashing of my computer on Bill Gates, who is the Antichrist.

APOCALYPSE

The devastating event—whether by supernatural forces, natural forces, or some sort of human action—that results in total destruction of society, the world, the universe, your kitchen sink, you name it. It's often used synonymously with the **Second Coming** of Christ. Occasionally it's used as another name for the New Testament book of **Revelation**. In fact, the word apocalypse comes from the Greek word *apokalypsis*, which means "the lifting of a veil"—a revelation. So now you know.

NOT TO BE CONFUSED WITH: Apocalypse, the immortal mutant supervillain in the Marvel Comics' Marvel Universe who didn't get along very well with the X-Men. (This entry applicable to comic book fanboys only.)

PLEASE USE IT IN A SENTENCE: I would prefer the Apocalypse to result from a wayward asteroid rather than nuclear holocaust, but I'm not saying why.

APOCALYPTIC LITERATURE

The name given to a specific genre of prophetic Jewish and Christian literature that flourished from around 200 B.C. to 200 A.D. This type of work usually features a revelatory dream or a cryptic end-of-the-world vision that touches on the coming kingdom of God and judgment of the dead. Apocalyptic literature tends to be dualistic, viewing everything as an ongoing battle between opposites—light and darkness, good and evil, God and Satan, Regis and Kelly. The best example of apocalyptic literature is the book of **Revelation**. The Old Testament book of **Daniel** can also be considered apocalyptic, as are several other ancient writings that didn't make the team, canonically speaking.

PLEASE USE IT IN A SENTENCE (OR TWO): Dude, this apocalyptic literature is freaking me out. Pass the Doritos.

ARMAGEDDON

According to Revelation 16:16, the final geographical location where the opposing armies of good (led by Christ) and evil (led by the **Antichrist**) clash in the biggest, baddest battle royale ever. Winner takes all. Armageddon is named after a hill near the town of Megiddo in Palestine, a site of many ancient battles. Often, the word Armageddon is used to refer more generally to the final good-versus-evil battle itself, and not just its location.

NOT TO BE CONFUSED WITH: *Armageddon* (1998), a fabulously expensive and dumb movie in which Bruce Willis and Ben Affleck are oil drillers who save the world from spectacular destruction via an out-of-control asteroid. Which itself is not to be confused with the movie *Deep Impact*, also released in 1998, in which Robert Duvall and other astronauts spectacularly fail to save the world from destruction via an asteroid. Which leads to a big tsunami and the unfortunate death of Téa Leoni.

PLEASE USE IT IN A SENTENCE: I'm so hungry, not even the forces of Armageddon could keep me away from that lobster bisque.

BABYLON

An evil city and immoral, idol-worshiping empire back in the day, used throughout the book of **Revelation** as a symbol for the early Roman Empire and its general skeeziness. Rome wasn't a good friend to early Christians, what with all the lions-versus-Christians battles getting top billing Friday nights at the Coliseum. So John, the author of Revelation, used a clever code to keep from openly harshing on his worst enemy, and everyone (except the Romans, apparently) knew it.

In later days, Babylon—also referred to as "The Great Harlot" in Revelation 17:5—has come to represent any nation or system that can be considered an enemy of God. A lot of fundamentalist Christians think this obviously means the Roman Catholic Church. Or Cold War-era Russia. Or the United Nations and its **New World Order**. Or even Hollywood with its secularity and liberal politics. And in recent years, word leaked out from Iraq that none other than Saddam Hussein was trying to rebuild and restore the ancient city of Babylon. Great bowls of wrath! So maybe John was being literal when he referred to Babylon instead of the wink-wink-this-is-really-Rome sneakiness. At any rate, Saddam's not doing much rebuilding these days. And according to Revelation, the symbolic Babylon gets it good in the end, suffering all kinds of godly wrath followed by utter destruction.

NOT TO BE CONFUSED WITH: Babylon 5, the best science fiction television show ever! (Or so the Pocket Guide is told.)

BEAST, THE

According to Revelation 13, another name for the **Antichrist**, who rules over people of every race, tribe, language, sexual orientation, and/or religious persuasion until Jesus comes back and straightens the place up. "The Beast" could also refer to the legendary supercomputer located in the headquarters of the Common Market in Brussels. It occupies three floors and can store the personal and financial information of up to two billion people, and has conveniently been nicknamed "The Beast" by wacky **eschatology**-minded employees. Newsflash, kids: Modern technology is greasing the wheel for the Antichrist's totalitarian rule. You've been warned.

SEE ALSO: Mark of the Beast

NOT TO BE CONFUSED WITH: Vincent, the underground monster/dreamlover (played by Ron Perlman in the late '80s television series *Beauty and the Beast*) who lived in the tunnels beneath New York City and, incidentally, had a soft spot for Linda Hamilton.

BEINGS, FOUR LIVING

Strange symbolic creatures said to surround the throne of God, as described in Revelation 4, Ezekiel 1, and Isaiah 6. The details in each of these passages are slightly different, but the one in **Revelation** is best known. It describes the first being as having the appearance of a lion. Another being looks like an ox. The third one sports the face of a man. And the fourth takes the form of a winged eagle. Each being is covered front and back with a multitude of eyes (yes, eyes) and has six wings. Day and night, the Four Living Beings proclaim God's holiness.

Due to the bizarre combo of eyes, wings, and other features, however, there is some disagreement about what, exactly, these creatures are. Ezekiel identifies them as *cherubim*, a special order of angels. Some modern theologians believe they symbolize the attributes of God—majesty and power (lion), faithfulness (ox), intelligence (human), and sovereignty (eagle). Others contend they represent the four major life forms on earth (wild animals, domestic animals, humans, and fowl). But most people just get stuck wigging out on all the eyeballs.

NOT TO BE CONFUSED WITH: The **Four Horsemen of the Apocalypse**, or the Four Great Beasts Who Rise Out of the Sea in Daniel 7. The latter are creatures similar to a winged lion, a flesh-devouring bear, a winged leopard, and a very scary horned creature that may or may not be the Antichrist.

BERNSTEIN, LEONARD

The only major American composer and symphony conductor whose name was recognizable to drunken frat boys of the late '80s and early '90s, as they were often heard shouting his name en masse during the third verse of REM's peppy "It's the End of the World as We Know It (And I Feel Fine)," from the 1987 album, *Document*.

PLEASE USE IT IN A SENTENCE: It is unlikely that Leonard Bernstein will play a major role, if any at all, in the final battle of good versus evil.

BOWLS OF WRATH, SEVEN

Plague-filled "bowls" (either very large or very symbolic) of God's final judgment, held and eventually poured out by seven angels onto the **Antichrist** and his followers. These are the last of three chronological seven-part judgments in **Revelation**, beginning with the **Seven Seals** and **Seven Trumpet Blasts**. Some believe this is part three of the **Tribulation**. But because they are very similar to the trumpet judgments, others theorize that the seals, trumpets, and bowls each describe the Tribulation in full—only with different imagery. An important distinction is that the **Seven Trumpet Blasts** only wipe out a third of the universe. With the bowls, destruction is total. But enough about that. Let's see what happens when each angel gets tipsy with his cosmic pottery:

● **BOWL 1**—Malignant sores break out over everyone sporting the **Mark of the Beast**.

● **BOWL 2**—The sea turns to blood, and everything in it dies.

◐ **BOWL 3**—Rivers and springs turn to blood.

◐ **BOWL 4**—The sun gets it this time, sending out a blast of heat that crispifies everything.

◑ **BOWL 5**—Poured over the throne of the Beast, this bowl plunges his kingdom into darkness and afflicts his followers with teeth-gnashing agony.

● **BOWL 6**—The Euphrates river dries up, allowing conquering armies to march over it without moistening so much as a pinky toe on their way to the battle of **Armageddon**.

◖ **BOWL 7**—Biggest. Earthquake. Ever. **Babylon** and other cities collapse into heaps. Islands disappear. Mountains are leveled. Thunder and lightning announce the arrival of the Mother of All Storms, which drops seventy-five-pound hailstones onto the remaining worshipers of the Antichrist, who really should have gotten the message by now.

CHILIASM

Belief in the Christian doctrine of the **millennium**, that the righteous will enjoy their rewards here on earth during Christ's thousand-year reign of peace.

PLEASE USE IT IN A SENTENCE: As if you're ever gonna need to use "chiliasm" in everyday conversation.

DANIEL, BOOK OF

The primary Jewish entry into **apocalyptic literature**, the book of Daniel details the apocalyptic visions and experiences Daniel had in the court of Nebuchadnezzar in **Babylon**, introducing, along the way, a bunch of the themes and symbols used in **Revelation**. Of primary prophetic importance (and endless discussion) is the book's description of "four great beasts" who arise from the sea in chapter 7. Also notable is a certain lion's den incident. Most contemporary scholars believe the book was written in the second century B.C. following the persecution of Israel by Antiochus Epiphanies of Syria. Which works for us.

PLEASE USE IT IN A SENTENCE: The book of Daniel also features the story of the fiery furnace, starring Shadrach, Meshach, and Abednego.

DISPENSATIONALISM

A Protestant theological system developed in the mid-1800s by English theologian John Nelson Darby, later popularized in the Scofield Reference Bible, first published in 1909. Dispensationalism divides history into separate epochs, called dispensations. Within each, God offers humanity a different avenue toward salvation. For instance, God's expectations and demands on the patriarchs of the Old Testament were different from his moral requirements on believers today. Dispensationalists are most likely conservative and/or fundamentalist evangelicals who believe in a literal interpretation of the Bible, a **premillennial Rapture**, and a distinction between God's plan for Israel and his dealings with the

Church. (*See chapter 5 for a more in-depth discussion of dispensational premillennialism.*)

PLEASE USE IT IN A SENTENCE: A majority of evangelical believers probably agree with the main tenets of dispensationalism, even though they don't have the slightest idea what the word means.

ELDERS

Described prominently in Revelation 4 and 5, the elders sit on thrones and worship God in heaven. There are twenty-four of them, each clothed in white and wearing a gold crown. There is some dispute as to whether the elders represent God's redeemed (twelve tribes of Israel + twelve apostles) or whether they are some sort of powerful members of the heavenly host who act as "assistants" to God. They may also allude to the twenty-four descendents of Aaron assigned by David to fulfill the role of chief priests in the new Temple. Or, what about the correlation to twenty-four hours in a day? Did anyone think of that?

NOT TO BE CONFUSED WITH: Pieter Bruegel the Elder, the great sixteenth century Flemish painter. Or, for that matter, Pliny the Elder (famed historian of ancient Rome) or Jocelyn Elder (former U.S. Surgeon General).

ESCHATOLOGY

The theological study of the end of human history, the fate of the world, the end of time, and so on. Almost every religion—from Norse paganism and its concept of **Ragnarok** to Zoroastrianism— has its own system of belief concerning The End. Christian eschatology focuses on the conclusion of God's purposes for mankind and the Church, bringing an end to history and resolving the pesky problem of evil. Also the belief that God will trounce

Satan in the final battle of **Armageddon**.

   NOT TO BE CONFUSED WITH: Scatology, the chemical analysis of excrement for medical diagnosis. There's an easy joke here somewhere . . . (rimshot!)

FEAST OF TRUMPETS

   Better known as Rosh Hashanah, the Jewish New Year. Doomies really like this date—and, honestly, any year will do—as a possibility for the **Rapture** due to the trumpet imagery. For the same reason, they also really like Wynton Marsalis.

HORSEMEN OF THE APOCALYPSE, FOUR

   The famous horsemen get their big shout-out in chapter 6 of Revelation upon the breaking of the first four of the **Seven Seals**. The riders are traditionally named War, Pestilence, Famine, and Death, but many scholars believe these may have been aliases. (Honestly, would it strike fear in your heart if the Horsemen of the Apocalypse were named Pete, Skip, Warren, and Buster? The Pocket Guide thinks not.)

   Horsey the First is white and ridden by a rider wielding a gut-shattering bow. He does a great deal of conquering. Next is a red horse, jockeyed by a rider with a mighty sword, who leaves a morbid trail of war and slaughter behind him. The third horse is black. Its rider carries a scale and delivers, well, a strongly worded statement about bread, barley, and olive oil. It's apparently a warning about famine, which just isn't nearly as intimidating as one would expect. (The black horse and rider probably get ribbed a lot by the other three.) And the fourth horse? Pale green, like a decaying corpse. Its rider is named Death (née Buster). The horsemen are given authority over a fourth of the earth, along with the freedom to spread violence and pestilence and devastation however they choose. But only within that 25 percent. No more or less. It's kind of a practice mini-judgment before the main event.

NOT TO BE CONFUSED WITH: The Four Horsemen of Notre Dame, the legendary football backfield of the Golden Dome's 1924 team, consisting of quarterback Harry Stuhldreher, fullback Elmer Layden, and halfbacks Jim Crowley and Don Miller. They were fine football players and all, but had very little dominion over the earth.

LEFT BEHIND

The bestselling series of novels by Tim LaHaye and Jerry Jenkins that fuse a pretribulationist, **premillennialist** theology of the **Second Coming** of Christ with the efficiently plotted narrative style of a contemporary thriller. Beginning just before the **Rapture** has taken place, the books—there will be sixteen in all, including three "countdown to the Rapture" titles (2005-2006) and a final installment (in 2007) about the last judgment—tell the story of Nicolae Carpathia, a Romanian president who ascends to secretary general of the United Nations, and then really gets down to business. He establishes world peace and disbands all military forces. He names himself "Potentate of the Global Community" (which sounds much better than the pithier, less popular "**Antichrist**"). Then he consolidates all the world's religions into a single faith with the teensy-bit-suspicious name of "Carpathianism." Which isn't good. Little Nicky is opposed by a handful of newly converted Christians (those left behind by the Rapture, natch) who call themselves the "Tribulation Force." Carpathia is also opposed by God. Who wins in book sixteen.

PLEASE USE IT IN A SENTENCE (OR TWO): Once I was really engrossed in reading book four of the Left Behind series at a coffee shop when I looked up and, like, all the customers had left and the guy behind the counter had gone into the back for some reason and I started to panic because what if the Rapture had just occurred and I had been "left behind" myself? But then I realized I hadn't heard a trumpet blast or anything. And the guy behind the counter eventually showed up again, so I felt better.

LOCUSTS

Scary little torture-machines loosed upon the world during the fifth **trumpet blast**. They come from the bottomless pit, led by their king, **Abaddon**, and are charged with the task of tormenting non-believers for five long months. These aren't your garden-variety locusts, either. They have human faces, long womanly hair, the teeth of a lion, bodies like horses, wings, and scorpion-like stingers. Many scholars think these "locusts" are actually demons. Which, in all honesty, makes a lot more sense, considering the jumbled Halloween costume appearance.

SEE ALSO: **Abaddon**; **Trumpet Blasts**, **Seven**
NOT TO BE CONFUSED WITH: Cicadas, the chirping-in-chorus insects that thrum in trees all over the eastern and southern United States, which are often incorrectly identified as "locusts." Or grasshoppers, which are called "locusts" in the Bible, but which are probably not demonic killers, and definitely don't have long, flowing hair, except in Disney movies.

MARK OF THE BEAST

More fun out of Revelation 13, which reveals that the **Antichrist** will require every man, woman, and child to receive a special "mark" on their right hand or forehead. Without the mark, you're all kinds of doomed. The markless can't buy or sell anything.

Not even on eBay.

Things get even more interesting in verse 18, when John—thought by most to be the author of **Revelation**—proclaims in his cryptic, I'm-having-a-freaky-vision custom, "Let the one who has understanding solve the number of the beast, for it is the number of a man. His number is 666."

Trust us, John. We've been working on it. The meaning of 666 has probably been pondered more than any other topic in Revelation. And that's really saying something. Some theories: 1) Throughout the Bible, seven is considered to be the perfect number. A trinity of sevens would therefore represent complete perfection. And three sixes? Would fall just short of complete perfection. Tricky! 2) The Greek letters corresponding to the name of the Roman Emperor Nero represent numbers that total 666. Which gives **Preterists** fits of glee. 3) How many letters in the name Ronald Wilson Reagan? Exactly: three names, six letters each. Could it be? (The Reagan-is-Antichrist theory held more water in the 1980s, primarily among Democrats. It has fallen significantly out of favor in the past few years.) (*Check out chapter 4 for more about the Mark of the Beast and the Antichrist.*)

SEE ALSO: Beast, The

PLEASE USE IT IN A SENTENCE (OR TWO): Triple sixes aside, it's hip now to attach the Mark of the Beast to bar code technology, with the Antichrist forcing everyone to get an invisible UPC code laser-tattooed onto their foreheads. In related news, hats will be discouraged during the Tribulation.

MILLENNIUM

A span of one thousand years. In apocalyptic terms, millennium refers to the thousand-year reign of Christ on earth, during which

Satan will be bound and cast into the bottomless pit, as described in Revelation 20. Most believers agree that Christ's reign will be one of peace, justice, well being, and happy kite-flying children. The big question is what the millennium is and when it will take place. Any day now? Far into the future? Is it literal? Is it a metaphor? This dispute has given us fun theories like **amillennialism**, **premillennialism**, and **postmillennialism**. A headache, too.

    SEE ALSO: Chiliasm

    NOT TO BE CONFUSED WITH: Millennium Hotels & Resorts, a London-based international chain of four-star deluxe properties, including twenty in North America. Christ also reigns in these hotels, but it's not as big of a deal.

NEW WORLD ORDER

So back in 1988, Mikhail Gorbachev (who was already considered a potential **Antichrist**, complete with a splotchy **Mark of the Beast**) used the phrase "New World Order" in an address to the United Nations, referring to a peaceful, internationally focused world no longer dominated by two opposing superpowers. Then U.S. President George H.W. Bush used the same phrase in a 1990 speech to Congress. The result? The apocalyptic went apoplectic (which is easy to do but hard to say). This New World Order, they figured, could be the evil worldwide government and/or religion foretold in the Bible, headed up by none other than the Antichrist. Conspiracy theorists jumped on this idea like fat kids on cake, and got all suspicious that a number of sinister End-Times players— including Jews, the Illuminati, the International Monetary Fund, the European Union, Freemasons, and even extra-terrestrials—were secretly planning behind the scenes to help get this one-world party started. Apparently they're still hard at work, as organizing a worldwide government can be a bureaucratic nightmare.

PLEASE USE IT IN A SENTENCE (OR TWO): My cable company just consolidated with an Internet provider! Just one more proof of the coming New World Order.

PAROUSIA

A debonair-sounding Greek word (literally, "presence") used by Christians to refer to the **Second Coming** of Christ at the End of Days. Jesus predicts his own comeback tour several times in the Gospels of Matthew, Luke, and John, saying that it will occur suddenly, like a lightning strike (Matt. 24:27). He couches it in vague, apocalyptic language, to the point that his disciples expected the return to happen during their lifetimes, and were greatly disappointed when it, um, didn't.

NOT TO BE CONFUSED WITH: Perusia, an ancient Etruscan city now known as Perugia, capital of the Umbria region of Italy. Yeah, okay. That one's a stretch.

POSTMILLENNIALISM

The belief that Jesus will hold off on his return engagement until humans have set up a happy, peaceful millennial kingdom on earth, accomplished gradually by converting humanity to faith in Christ, according to God's plan. In its milder forms, postmillennialism seems pretty reasonable. You get hopeful folks like the Puritans, who try to build a righteous society via progressive reforms, or utopian communities like those of the Shakers. On the other hand, you get crazies—like the sixteenth century German Anabaptist Thomas Muentzer (*see chapter 2*)—who prefer to bring God's kingdom to earth via violent theocracy. At any rate, belief in postmillennialism has played an important role in history, as it typically leads to a fair amount of social change. Or in the case of Muentzer, a fair amount of massacre. (*See chapter 5 for more about postmillennialism.*)

PLEASE USE IT IN A SENTENCE: Because it sees the world as gradually becoming a better place, postmillennialism is not a popular position to hold during times of war.

~~PREMILLENNIALISM~~

The belief that God's **millennial** kingdom won't occur until after Jesus returns visibly and in person to save humanity and wipe the satanic smirk off Beelzebub's piehole. Unlike its cousin, **postmillennialism**, premillennialism fosters a doom-and-gloom kind of mentality: The world's getting a whole lot more wicked (the bad kind of wicked, as opposed to, say, "wicked hardcore"), so it's a good thing Jesus is coming back. Premills envision the perfect, future millennial reign of Christ as an antidote to the suffering and evil in today's society. Because God is in charge of eventually fixing the place up, **premillennialists** may be less concerned with planetary upkeep—not as much social action, less non-proselytizing interest in one's fellow man, little concern for the environment (to make a sweeping generalization). Instead, they're more into personal evangelism and preparing for Christ's return, which is why premills get all nervy about stuff like the **Rapture** and the **Tribulation** and possible fulfillments of prophecy, assuming that events of the present are divine signs of future Apocalypse. (*See chapter 5 for a more in-depth discussion of premillennialism.*)

PLEASE USE IT IN A SENTENCE: Because it views the world as being on a speedboat to hell, premillennialism is a popular theory during times of war.

PRETERISM

The doctrine or belief system that maintains that most biblical prophecies—especially those related to the End Times—have already been fulfilled, either in the person of Jesus Christ or in the destruction of the **Temple** in the late first century. For instance, the dire predictions of Christ on the Mount of Olives in Matthew 24 ("The sign of the coming of the Son of Man will appear in the heavens . . .") refer to the events surrounding the destruction of the Jewish Temple by Roman armies in 70 A.D., which included plenty of slaughter, war, fire, and despair.

PLEASE USE IT IN A SENTENCE (OR TWO): Taking Preterism one step further, I believe not only does New Testament prophecy find its fulfillment in the destruction of the Temple, but so does every fortune cookie message the Pocket Guide has ever received. Like, how obvious is: "You will be happy socially and in your work"?

RAGNAROK

In Norse mythology, the final battle at the end of the world, between the gods (led by chief executive god Odin) and the fire giants and fearsome wolves and miscellaneous other monsters led by a shape-shifting trickster spirit named Loki. When the dust clears, everyone's dead—the gods included—and the entire universe has been ripped to shreds. Utter destruction. We're hoping it doesn't come to that.

NOT TO BE CONFUSED WITH: The online role-playing game of the same name, which, technically, doesn't bring about universal destruction and/or chaos. Though there are probably a handful of cheat codes that let you come close.

RAPTURE, THE

The belief that true, faithful followers of Jesus Christ will be physically "lifted up" to heaven prior to the **Second Coming**. Beliefs about the Rapture are based on 1 Thessalonians 4:16-17, in which the Apostle Paul describes believers being "caught up in the air" when the trumpets sound. The Rapture is a fundamental element of **premillennial dispensationalist** belief systems, though not everyone agrees when to cue the heavenly horn section. Most think it will occur prior to the seven-year **Tribulation** period, thereby sparing Christians all the bad mojo those left behind are sure to experience. Others believe the Rapture will occur in the middle of the Tribulation, after the **Antichrist** has come to power but before all the really bad stuff starts to go down. Some even schedule it to occur with Christ's return at the end of the Tribulation period—which puts believers in the same horrific boat as everyone else. Crikey. So you have pre-trib, mid-trib, and post-trib premillennialists. And you thought distinguishing between the two Darrens on *Bewitched* was tricky.

NOT TO BE CONFUSED WITH: The Second Coming, or ***parousia***, which is a separate event that won't occur until after the Tribulation. Unless you're a post-tribulationist, which means you believe the Rapture and Christ's return will probably be simultaneous. If that's the case, you are free to confuse the two.

PLEASE USE IT IN A SENTENCE (OR TWO): Many premillennialists have clever bumper stickers that read, "In case of Rapture, this car will be unmanned." Because chaos on the interstate highway system is hilarious when viewed from heaven.

REVELATION, BOOK OF

The final entry in the New Testament and annual winner of

the "Most Controversial Book of the Bible" award, and the poster child of **apocalyptic literature**. Historically authored by the Apostle John (though some scholars dispute this) and detailing his disturbing vision of the End of Days, Revelation is believed to have been written in the final years of the first century following the 70 A.D. destruction of the **Temple** (or, if you're a **Preterist**, a few years before the destruction of the Temple). Despite the difficulty of its imagery, Revelation is the guidebook for students of Christian **eschatology**, and the endless source of **Rapture**-predicting, **Antichrist**-designating, and general end-of-the-worldliness.

In fact, the events described in Revelation are so entrenched in our culture that many of them have made the leap from arcane eschatological lingo to common vernacular. So you have people who don't know the Bible from the Bhagavad-Gita, but they do know 666 is the **Mark of the Beast**. And they've heard of the **Seventh Seal**, and the **Four Horsemen of the Apocalypse**, and the Whore of **Babylon**. Filling in the gaps is why this glossary exists, thankyouverymuch.

PLEASE USE IT IN A SENTENCE: Many Christians see the book of Revelation as a blueprint for the Last Days of the universe, including Tim LaHaye, who also sees it as a killer plot device.

SEALS, SEVEN

The first of three seven-part judgments in the book of **Revelation**, along with the **Seven Trumpet Blasts** and the **Seven Bowls of Wrath**. Each seal is broken—and set loose upon the world—by Christ the Lamb. In chapter 6, the first four seals release the **Four Horsemen of the Apocalypse**. The fifth reveals the souls of martyrs crying for judgment. The sixth seal is pretty serious, discharging universal catastrophe: earthquakes, meteors, darkening of the sun and moon, people hiding in caves from the wrath of God, and so forth. The seventh seal brings a half-hour of much-needed silence ... eventually shattered by the Seven Trumpet Blasts.

Some consider the seals to be a chronology of the entire **Tribulation**, culminating in Christ's return. Others think they're just part of a whole series of badness—continuing with the trumpets and wrath bowls—leading up to the Day of the Lord.

SEE ALSO: **Trumpet Blasts, Seven**; **Bowls of Wrath, Seven**

PLEASE USE IT IN A SENTENCE: My sister kept talking about how cool the Seven Seals were, which seemed really morbid until I found out she'd been to SeaWorld.

SECOND COMING

See **Parousia**.

TEOTWAWKI

An acronym for "the end of the world as we know it," used as shorthand by all the cool kids in the End-Times gang.

NOT TO BE CONFUSED WITH: Téa Leoni, the actress who starred in the apocalyptic asteroid-hits-the-earth movie *Deep Impact* (1998).

TEMPLE, THE

In Old Testament times, the most sacred place in Israel. In the End Times, the most important piece of real estate in the world.

The temple was built by Solomon around 950 B.C. and became the central place for the people of Israel to worship God and make sacrifices. It was destroyed by those nefarious Babylonians in 587 B.C., then rebuilt, then razed again during the Roman-Jewish War in 70 A.D. (an event Jesus predicts in Matthew 24). Today, its former location—the Temple Mount in the heart of modern Jerusalem—is partially occupied by the Dome of the Rock, an Islamic holy site. This irritates the Jewish people, who, honestly, have been through quite enough when it comes to their most sacred place.

Unfortunately, things will only get worse, prophetically speaking. According to the book of **Daniel**, the **Antichrist** will set up shop in a restored Temple, desecrating it by claiming to be God. This is supposed to happen midway through the **Tribulation**. Which means the Temple will need to be restored right about the same time the world Tribs out. Which means Apocalypse watchers are biting their nails looking for guys wearing hardhats and consulting blueprints in the vicinity of the Temple Mount. Which means you may now add church architects to the Harbingers of Doom list.

PLEASE USE IT IN A SENTENCE (OR TWO): The location of the ancient Jewish Temple is now home to the spectacular Mosque of Omar, more commonly known as the Dome of the Rock. Mainly because "Omar" is a pretty goofy name.

TRIBULATION

According to most **premillennial** viewpoints, a seven-year period of intense, worldwide suffering following the **Antichrist**'s rise to power. The seven years are usually divided into two sections, 3.5 years apiece. In the first half, the Antichrist sets up a one-world government (a.k.a. **New World Order**?) and fools the world into thinking he's establishing peace. In the second half, he goes around making Hitler and Stalin look like a bunch of grandmothers baking bunny-shaped cookies. During the Tribulation, everyone on earth will die, wiped out by wars, plagues, famine, earthquakes, death rays from space, and all-around mayhem. Only a small number of faithful believers—those who converted to Christianity after being left behind by the **Rapture**—will survive. There is much hardship, torture, and gnashing of teeth until **Armageddon**, when Christ's defeat of the Antichrist ushers in the earthly millennial kingdom. Thank God. (*See chapter 5 for a more in-depth discussion of the Tribulation.*)

PLEASE USE IT IN A SENTENCE: Because the Tribulation doesn't sound very fun, I'm voting for a pre-trib Rapture.

TRUMPET BLASTS, SEVEN

The second of three seven-part judgments in **Revelation**, beginning with the **Seven Seals** and ending with the **Seven Bowls of Wrath**. The trumpet blasts, released with the opening of the seventh seal, could be part two of the **Tribulation**. Or they could just be a recap of the previously mentioned Seven Seals, which some believe detail the whole Tribbie enchilada in full. Either way, these aren't happy, jazzy trumpets. A quick breakdown:

ONE—Hail and fire mixed with blood (what?!?) destroy a third of the earth's vegetation.

TWO—A mountain of fire falls into the sea, turning it to blood and offing a third of its creatures and even ships and sailors.

THREE—A great flaming star (a meteor, mind you, as opposed to a gay celebrity) falls from the sky, poisoning a third of the world's rivers and springs. This is an important star, as it has a name: Bitterness, or Wormwood.

FOUR—No less than a third of the universe bites it. One-third of the sun, one-third of the moon, one-third of the stars.

FIVE—Another star falls from the sky, this one with a key in his pocket. (Yes, a star wearing pants. Stay with us here.) Starpocket opens a closet in the bottomless pit and looses killer **Locusts** who are charged with terrorizing non-believers for five long months, led by **Abaddon**.

SIX—Four angels of death are released, along with an army of 200 million mounted troops, to kill one-third of all the people on earth. They ride lion-headed horses with really awful breath—fire and smoke and burning sulfur billow from their mouths—which ends up killing a lot of people. They also have tails with snake heads, resulting in additional damage while upping the freakiness quotient.

SEVEN—The return of Christ amid flashing lightning, roaring thunder, hail-a-plenty, and a big earthquake.

WITNESSES, TWO

Revelation 11:3 tells of two powerful human prophets who will stand up against the evil of the Last Days and give a final warning to the citizens of earth, calling for worldwide repentence. The two are also able to defend themselves by spewing fire from their mouths. And turning rivers and oceans to blood. And smiting the world's population, when necessary, with plagues. Needless to say, these witnesses are not the most popular kids on the playground, despite being on the side of the Almighty during the whole good-versus-evil final conflict. The Beast from the bottomless pit eventually pops up to kill them, which causes the people of the world to rejoice and throw a big party because finally the troublemakers are gone. And this witness-exterminating **Antichrist**/Beast guy? He's an okay dude! He should run for office or something.

Silly people of the world.

PLEASE USE IT IN A SENTENCE (OR TWO): There were two witnesses to my mother-in-law's car accident, but they weren't the fire-flashing ones from the Bible. However, one of them did have pretty oniony breath.

THE END IS NEAR,
PART I (A TIMELINE: 2000 B.C. UNTIL 1900)

Doomsaying has been a favorite pastime of, oh, just about everyone since the first ancient prophets discovered a timeless secret: By mixing a loud voice with passionate descriptions of the world's end, one can gather a substantial crowd. Maybe even a cult-like following. At the least, a willing groupie or two. Here, then, are some of the most notable apocalyptic predictions from way, way back, beginning in biblical times and continuing until the twentieth century rolls around. Most of them were wrong. At least so far.

2000-1500 B.C., PERSIA:

Think apocalyptic prophecy begins and ends with the Bible? Think again. The granddaddy of doomsday predictions is none other than the world's foremost Z-named religious figure: Zoroaster. Also known as Zarathustra.[1] Possibly a contemporary of Abraham, Zoroaster doubles as a nomadic tribesman and religious prophet in the region we now know as Iran. When his people find themselves surrounded on all sides by a number of bullying tribes, the Z-Man decides they need some divine intervention. He worships a number of gods, of course, but the foremost one is Ahura Mazda, which sounds like a car dealership but probably isn't. Anyway, Zoroaster produces some religious literature and poetry that appeal for the Mazda god to intervene in a cosmic final-battle-of-good-versus-evil kind of way, in order to save the good people and annihilate the bad ones. The final result is supposed to be a perfect, heaven-on-earth world for the good guys. There are still a few Zoroastrians around these days (140,000 or so), mainly in Iran and India. They're still waiting patiently for blood-soaked annihilation, and mostly drive Miatas.

634 B.C., ROME:

As the legend goes, Romulus, the founder of Rome, hears from twelve mystical eagles that are supposed to represent the lifetime of his great city. Early Romans hypothesize that each eagle represents a decade. Rome was founded in 753 B.C., so 120 years later—according to, you know, the eagles—the great empire becomes toast. There is much despair until nothing happens in that 120th year. Then there is much revision.

---

1. Zoroaster is the name the ancient Greeks gave to Zarathustra, but in modern days, Zoroaster is preferred. For one thing, the religious tradition named after him is called Zoroastrianism. Which is hard enough to say anyway. "Zarathustrianism" is well nigh impossible. For the record, Nietzsche was a fan of the original name, titling one of his most famous books *Thus Spake Zarathustra*. Just a little water cooler trivia for you.

389 B.C., ROME:

That whole "one mystical eagle equals ten years of Roman glory" idea? Rubbish. Symbolism experts get canned. New consultants come in. They decide that each eagle symbolizes one month out of the year. Back then, the official calendar stretches ten months to the year, so the expected downfall of society is reforecasted for 389 B.C. Unfortunately, it comes and goes in the middle of the Roman Republic's Golden Age. So much for prophetic birds of prey.

167 B.C., BABYLON:

The first in a long line of apocalyptic literature, the Book of Daniel is written while the Jews are being persecuted under the Syro-Greek rule of the Seleucids (commonly referred to as the Antiochian persecution, just so you'll know). The book features five dreams/revelations that detail what is to come in the Last Days, including troop movements, invasions, etc. In Daniel's vision, God's chosen people win, and the enemies of the Almighty are defeated. Which, thematically, is not too different from Zoroaster's version of the end game, except Daniel makes the cut for the Old Testament.

70 A.D., JERUSALEM:

In the Gospel of Mark (believed to have been written forty years or so after the death of Christ), Jesus gives his disciples a preview of The End, predicting wars, rumors of wars, earthquakes, and famine. "I tell you the truth," he says, "this generation will certainly not pass away until all these things have happened." Many of His contemporaries understand this literally and are disappointed when his Second Coming fails to materialize within their lifetimes. In the same passage, Jesus also cautions against date-setting. "No one knows about that day or hour," he says, "not even the angels in heaven." Everyone pretty much ignores this last part for the next two thousand years or so.

90 A.D., PATMOS:

The Apostle John, in exile on the isle of Patmos, has a vision of the end of the world. Once written, it becomes the New Testament book of Revelation. Perhaps you've heard of it.

156 A.D., PHRYGIA:

So this ascetic guy named Montanus starts speaking in tongues and making prophecies and calling himself the incarnation of the Holy Spirit. All blasphemy aside, he gains a bunch of followers. Then he picks up a couple of secondary seers/groupies named Maximilla and Priscilla who start harmonizing with him on his "The End is near" predictions, and, before you know it, the world's first Christian doomsday cult has hit the market. Among other things, the Montanists believe Christ will return within their lifetimes and that the New Jerusalem will drop from heaven right there onto Pepuza, in the land of Phrygia (modern-day Turkey). This never comes to pass, but Montanism flourishes for several more centuries. And Pepuza? Fun to say.

365 A.D., GAUL:

A fellow with the unfortunately dainty name of Hilary of Poitiers (and the equally unfortunate Latin name of, heh heh, Hilarius) gets all into finger-pointing the Antichrist and predicting The End. He schedules it for 365. Then he takes it back when 366 rolls around. That doesn't keep him, however, from reaching sainthood in the 1800s.

500 A.D.:

A nice round number. Surely Jesus will return during a year with a nice round number. So believes noted three-named theologian Sextus Julius Africanus. And Hippolytus. And Irenaeus, too. But not Jesus.

APRIL 6, 793 A.D., SPAIN:

Beatus, an elderly Spanish monk, gets really plucky one day and, amid a crowd of people, prophesies on April 6 that the Second Coming of Christ will occur this very day! So everyone commences freaking out and fasting and generally making panicky noises until the sun comes up on April 7. And seeing that everyone is still present, including Beatus, they all go home and eat.[2]

950 A.D., FRANCE:

What's with these European monks? Adso of Montiers writes a thrilling End-Times treatise for a certain Queen Gerberga, sister of Germany's Emperor Otto the Great. In it, Adso predicts the rise of the Antichrist—establishing the idea of a "last world emperor"—which he expects to happen as soon as the line of French kings dwindles away. The letter spreads throughout Europe and becomes very influential, eschatologically speaking. Which is one reason you have so many kids these days named "Adso."

968 A.D., EUROPE:

Major solar eclipse. Major apocalyptic panic. Major jumping to conclusions. Same old story.

989 A.D., EUROPE:

Halley's Comet. See above.

---

2. Beatus goes on to re-prophesy the end of the world, this time for the year 800. He still gets it wrong. But he dies in 798, so it's no biggie.

DECEMBER 31, 999 A.D. / JANUARY 1, 1000 A.D., ROME:

If you think we contemporary, technologically savvy urban sophisticates got worked up about Y2K, you shoulda been around back when the last millennium rolled over! Actually, not really. Despite what we've all been told, there probably wasn't much of a Y1K hoo-ha. Why? Because, this being smack in the middle of the Dark Ages, no one—save a few lucky clerics—can read a lick. Or tell you what year it is, either (desk calendars hadn't yet been invented). Or spell "millennia." Sure, a few bookish monks get their cassocks in a wad. And Pope Sylvester presides over a fairly histrionic crowd of pilgrims attending midnight mass at St. Peter's on New Year's Eve. But that's it.

1033 A.D.:

See, everyone was wrong! The Second Coming won't occur a thousand years from the birth of Christ, but from his death. Or so a few think. But still no dice. No Christ, either.

1186 A.D., SPAIN:

In 1179, a guy named John of Toledo, who has been spending far too much time fidgeting with his telescope, calculates that there will be a portentous alignment of planets in seven years. He prints up all these pamphlets and whips up a reasonable stew of hysteria. The dreaded year 1186 arrives. People hide in caves. The Emperor of Constantinople walls up his windows. The Archbishop of Canterbury calls for a day of atonement. Nothing happens. Toledo John legally changes his name to John of Cincinnati and goes into hiding.

1260 A.D., ITALY:

Way back in the late 1100s, this mystic named Joachim of Fiore receives a handful of revelations from his personal deity. He, ahem, "learns" that the Antichrist is already in the world, that King Richard of England will defeat him, and that the new millennium will begin sometime between 1200 and 1260. Which is a pretty big window of opportunity, if you ask the Pocket Guide, but the Big Show still doesn't come to pass. His followers (the Joachites) reschedule the End of Days for 1290.[3]

1346 A.D., EUROPE:

The Black Plague ravishes Europe, killing a third of its population. Doomsday for sure, as chaos reigns and everyone begins to suspect The End is near. Same goes for 1347. And 1348. More plaguey trouble in 1349, too. And so on, until the plague has run its course and everyone feels better again.

1420 A.D., CZECH REPUBLIC:

The Taborites, a radical wing of the Hussite movement—which in itself was a nice little religious reform sect—decide the credits are about to roll on Planet Earth. So they set up a utopian community around Mount Tabor in Bohemia (south of Prague). That is, if by "utopia" you mean "a place where you go full-bore military and take up arms against your oppressors." And burn down Catholic churches, too. (According to the Taborite code, the Catholic Church was the Whore of Babylon, and the pope was the Antichrist.) The whole Taborite thing kind of lost momentum, however, when more moderate Hussites defeated them in 1434. If by "defeated them" you mean "burned them as heretics."

3. And then again for 1335. If at first you don't succeed …

1504 A.D., ITALY:

Florentine Renaissance painter Sandro Botticelli finishes his famous *The Mystical Nativity*. Mystical is right—the painting has a quirky Greek caption, which reads, in part: "I Sandro painted this picture at the end of the year 1500 in the troubles of Italy in the half time after the time according to the eleventh chapter of St. John in the second woe of the Apocalypse in the loosing of the devil for three and a half years. Then he will be chained in the twelfth chapter and we shall see him trodden down as in this picture." Nice. Ol' Sandro figures he's living during the Tribulation, and the millennium is due in a good three-and-a-half years. Um, Sandro? Stick with painting.[4]

1516, ITALY:

The Catholic Church goes on the offensive with the Fifth Lateran Council, which issues a decree on preaching and prophecy directed at clerics who receive and promote direct revelation from God. Specifically, good Christians are prohibited from predicting in their sermons "any fixed time of future evils, of Antichrist's coming, or the day of Last Judgment." Not everyone gets the memo.

FEBRUARY 1, 1524, LONDON:

Taking cues from Noah (and conveniently ignoring the whole rainbow promise), a few London astrologers decide floods are all the rage. They calculate that the world will come to a soggy end on February 1. And since those cute little inflatable arm floaties are still a few centuries from hitting the shelves, panic sets in. Something like twenty thousand people abandon their homes for higher ground. The prior of St. Bart's builds a fortress and stockpiles food and water (so much for serving your fellow man). Then February

34   4. It is at this point in the chapter that we're going to lose the "A.D." designation, which tends to clutter up the headings. Welcome, everyone, to the Common Era.

1 rolls around dry as a bone, which just never happens in England. Ever. Apparently, the astrologers botched the math, because they later decide the Big Flood will come in 1624. See why it's so important to carry the one?

1525, GERMANY:

Add Thomas Muentzer to the list of thorns in the side of the establishment. A grumpy German Anabaptist and former student of Luther, Muentzer thinks he's living during "the end of all ages." He is also fiercely egalitarian and starts up a peasants' revolt in Thuringia, complete with pitchforks and everything. He tells his thousands of followers that God has guaranteed victory against the rich and powerful (i.e. the German army)—in fact, the Almighty will personally intervene to make sure everyone stays safe-and-sound. Besides, Muentzer promises, he will personally catch the army's cannonballs in the sleeves of his cloak. It's not bragging if you can back it up, you know. But Tommy can't. His army comes to a bloody end, as does his neck after he's beheaded.

1535, GERMANY:

More wiggy Anabaptist fun, inspired by Muentzer's shenanigans. Dude named Jan Matthys starts bossing around folks in the town of Munster, which, incidentally, he has declared to be the New Jerusalem. Then he dies leading a raid on Easter Sunday, the day they believe the world will end. So another Jan, this one by the name of Bockelson, takes his place as wacked-out Munster master. Jan Bockelson declares himself "Messiah of the Last Days" and unnerves the townspeople by running around naked in a state of ecstasy. And instituting the practice of polygamy. And minting money with helpful apocalyptic sayings on it. And requiring his followers to maintain vows of poverty while he prances around living the high life. Eventually Catholic/Lutheran forces break through the town walls and capture the deranged Bockelson, locking him in a cage in the town square and slowly torturing him.[5]

1537, FRANCE:

Astrologer Pierre Turrell combines the ancient arts of gutsy calamity-predicting and cowardly arse-covering by calculating four possible dates of doom: 1537, 1544, 1801, and 1814. He's careful to keep his list unpublished until he dies, though. Which makes dealing with the consequences much easier. Shut up, Pierre.

APRIL 28, 1583, LONDON:

Since the flood thing didn't pan out, London astronomers turn to another force of nature. They decide the world's end will be brought on by a mighty wind. Shut up, astronomers.

1600, GERMANY:

Our friend Martin Luther throws his floppy black hat into the doomsaying ring. He goes on record saying the world's expiration date hits no later than this year. But he was more of a reformer than a prophet, so cut him some slack.

1603, ITALY:

A Franciscan monk by the name of Tomasso Campanella predicts the sun will collide with the earth. Which is a good thing, he says, because it will burn all our sins away and usher in the reign of the Messiah. Tomasso was no scientist, though, so he tries to enlist none other than Galileo to help him do some calculations. Galileo calculates that Tomasso is a few gases short of a flaming sphere and

5. By the way, religious bigwigs like Luther and Calvin were quick to distance themselves from all the Anabaptist weirdness in Thuringia and Munster. Beheadings and slow public torture being a fairly good deterrent.

refuses to get involved. Another good thing, because the Church ships Tomasso off to the pokey for being a heretic.

1650, ENGLAND:

Anglican Bishop James Ussher publishes *The Annals of the Old Testament, Deduced from the First Origin of the World*. In it, he adds up all the "begats" and numbered life spans from the Bible and concludes that God flipped the Creation switch four thousand years before Christ. Like many back then, he assumes the course of human history will last six thousand years (based on the six days of Creation). So four thousand B.C. plus six thousand years places the Big Event in the year 2000. Ussher didn't stick around to see if it all panned out, but his 6K chronology still lives on today, especially among fundamentalist Christians and "Young Earth" creationists.

1666, ENGLAND:

Take the thousand years of a millennium, add to it the number of the Beast from Revelation (666), and you've got yourself a serviceable date for the Second Coming! The Brits get all nervous, especially when nasty omens like civil war, another bout with the plague, and the Great Fire of London start piling up during the year. Where's a good flood when you need it?

Also in 1666, a Jewish mystic named Shabbetai Tzevi goes all Kabbalah-kooky. Even more so than Madonna. Seems he declared himself Messiah back in 1648 and gained a rabble of followers. Which isn't anything we haven't seen before, until you find out that he convinced these followers that he would personally be leading the chosen people back into Israel while riding on the back of a giant lion with a seven-headed dragon in its jaws. Not even Siegfried & Roy in their prime could have pulled that off.

Anyway, Tzevi schedules the lion-riding for 1666, until he goes and gets excommunicated by the rabbis of Jerusalem. So he caravans to Constantinople and starts making demands on the Sultan. Not one to take orders from a guy named Shabbetai—even if he claims to be the Messiah—the Sultan takes the key and locks him up, giving him a choice: Convert to Islam or convert to headlessness. The Shabster chooses Allah, and this distresses his followers, who just aren't cool with a Muslim Messiah. A few hardcores remain, though, and Shabbetaianism carries over into the next century. Personally, the Pocket Guide is still waiting to see that dragon-chomping monster lion. Because, cool.

FALL OF 1694, AMERICA:

Ah, progress . . . The Apocalypse reaches the New World! German prophet Johann Jacob Zimmerman figures The End will arrive this year, and the epicenter will be none other than Germantown, Pennsylvania. (Funny. Was this part of God's plan all along? Was he just waiting for the town to be settled, or what?) Anyhow, J.J. recruits a bunch of groupies to join him in welcoming Jesus back to earth, but then dies on the day of departure. Worst. Timing. Ever. Nonplussed, Johannes Kelpius, your run-of-the-mill cave-dwelling mystic, takes over as cruise director. They land in America and proceed to transmogrify into a cult known as "The Women in the Wilderness." Not sure where the "women" part comes from, most of them being male, but, you know, to each his own. Kelpius and the girls fast, pray, and generally wait for the trumpet blast. It never happens. They finally realize Jesus is on, like, a whole different timeline. Being stood up is tough anyway, but when your date is Jesus? Heartbreaking. The disconsolate women return to Germany.

MAY 19, 1719, SWITZERLAND:

Famed mathematician Jakob Bernoulli (you know him for his groundbreaking calculus papers on transcendental curves and isoperimetry—or perhaps you don't) applies his number-crunching genius to a new equation: the chance a comet will bring about the world's end. Seems a suspicious candidate had been spied back in 1680, so Jake predicts it'll return in apocalyptic fashion on the precise date above. I'd blame him for shoddy math, but the guy's a freakin' genius. So chalk this one up to plain old delusion.

1736, AMERICA:

A highly influential Puritan preacher with the hobbit-like name of Cotton Mather sets this year as the start of Christ's comeback tour. Of course, he said the same thing back in 1697—portraying himself as leading the final charge against the devil's legions—and then again in 1716. You'd think the guy would eventually get the idea and keep his date-setting lips zipped. But then you'd be wrong.[6]

1776, BOSTON:

You know all those cool stories about the Boston Tea Party and the Declaration of Independence and Paul Revere? What you probably haven't heard is that behind the scenes of the American Revolution is a healthy dose of End-Times mania. You have rebel-rousing pamphleteers equating the sinister Stamp Act with Revelation's Mark of the Beast. A few ambitious souls proclaim King George to be the Antichrist. And when the war ends, preachers get all yappy about the United States being Christ's new millennial kingdom. Guess we're still working on that one.

---

6. Incidentally, ol' Cotton played a substantial role in the Salem Witch Trials in 1692. Three of the five judges who heard evidence were members of his church and personal friends. Which is only marginally related to the subject at hand, but interesting all the same.

1792, UPSTATE NEW YORK:

The Shakers, an offshoot of the Quakers, start calling themselves the "Millennial Church" and attracting followers to a commune near Albany.[7] They're named for their calorie-burning practice of dancing and trembling during worship services, an activity they believe can purge sin from their bodies. Whatever. If that were the case, Charo would be pope. Anyhow, their founder, a certain Mother Ann Lee, is convinced she and her followers will usher in the new millennium, and quick. At least they hope so, since being a Shaker requires a vow of celibacy. And also a proficiency at building tasteful wooden furniture.

1809, ENGLAND:

There's this highly esteemed fortuneteller in Yorkshire who has a magic chicken. Her name is Mary Bateman. (The fortuneteller, that is. Not the chicken. Stay with us here.) Lo and behold, the tricksy bird has the ability to lay prophetic eggs. Grunt, squawk, squeeze, and out pops an egg with a message written on it . . . as if by magic! Eventually, an Extra Large comes out with the Grade-A warning that Jesus is a-coming, soon and very soon. The public bum-rushes her place to get a gander at the Chicken of Doom. But someone peeks in before the curtain rises and sees Mary trying to, um, shove an egg up the chicken's pooper. So much for apocalyptic poultry. Mary goes out of business, and eats scrambled eggs along with her crow.

1830, NEW ENGLAND:

Visions, the angel Moroni, gold plates, and suddenly this failed farmer named Joseph Smith has a direct line to God the Father and Jesus Christ his Son. An ambitious fellow, Smith rolls out the Book

7. Back in England, they were called the "Shaking Quakers." Which, in terms of redundancy, is like being called a funny comedian.

of Mormon and gets to work restoring the "true" church. And the "true" believers? They're Smitty's Latter Day Saints and will have the privilege of reigning with Christ during the coming millennium. Oh, and also? Dude hears this mysterious voice and interprets it as saying that Jesus won't return until Joseph turns eighty-five years old in 1890. The fact that Joe gets murdered by a mob in 1844 puts a significant kink in the plans. But Mormonism continues to flourish.

1844, NEW YORK & MASSACHUSETTS:

Hoo boy. This ex-Army-captain-turned-Baptist-preacher named William Miller—founder, conveniently enough, of the Millerite movement—starts up a fire-and-brimstone show. Heavy on the fire. Jesus will return and the faithful will be raptured, he predicts, sometime between March 21, 1843, and March 21, 1844, after which the world will burn with the white-hot intensity of a thousand suns. Or something to that effect. He attracts an estimated 100,000 disciples and/or hopped-up pyros. Newspapers report these followers giving away all their possessions, abandoning their jobs and homes, and refusing to plant or harvest crops. Which gives them more time to contemplate the just-about-nigh Rapture and speak in tongues and thrash around in spiritual ecstasy. There are also stories of some really devout Millerites jumping from rooftops in an attempt to time their leaps with the Rapture. (Who knew the Apocalypse sparked the first vestiges of extreme sports?) Everybody gets really feverish as March 21 approaches. Then really, really upset when March 22 hits. So Miller bites the bullet and owns up to his mistake . . . just a little bit. Because he quickly sets October 22 as the real Rapture date. For sure this time. Everyone gets goosebumpy again, and the craziness builds to a fevered pitch. When the big day (part deux) arrives, hoards of Millerites gather together to wait for the Messiah, arms outstretched, praying and swaying and singing and waiting for the closing bell. Long story short: October 23 brings what history has deemed "The Great Disappointment." The Millerites are rocked by a major group downer. Depression sets in. Thousands leave the movement. Those who stay eventually morph into Second Day Adventists and Seventh-Day Adventists.[8]

1863, ENGLAND:

Self-appointed prophet John Wroe joins a long list of loonies by predicting The End's arrival in 1863. And guess what? He's even freakier than your basic garden-variety apocalyptic prognosticator. Described as a small, wiry hunchback, legend has it Wroe made two attempts to walk on water (neither successful) and invited the public to nothing less than his own circumcision, as a full-grown adult. Yeah, ewwww.

1874, PENNSYLVANIA:

Another Millerite offshoot, the Jehovah's Witnesses (though they won't officially call themselves that until 1931), flare up under the leadership of Charles Taze Russell. Chuckie T. declares that Jesus and Armageddon will both come knocking in 1874. He reaches this conclusion based on studies of the Bible and the Great Pyramid. Yes, that Great Pyramid. When the year passes without incident, his apocalyptic predicting takes a creative turn. No, no, wait, says Charles. You don't understand. Jesus did come back in 1874, but he's invisible and hasn't chosen to reveal himself yet. Besides, only those with powerful "eyes of faith" can see him. You can guess where this is going: None of his followers are willing to admit to weak faith-vision, so no one questions the whole invisible Jesus scenario.

---

8. Seems those crazy Second Day Adventists couldn't get enough of the prophesying. They predicted 1845, then 1846, then 1849, and, finally, 1851 as possible dates for the Second Coming. That's a lot of disappointment for one group to handle.

Russell and the Watchtower Bible and Tract Society (the publishing arm of the Jehovah's Witnesses) become quite adept at predicting the Lord's return, as we shall soon see.

1900, BRAZIL:

Way up in the badlands of northeast Brazil, an elderly mystic named Antonio Conselheiro (rough translation: Counselor Tony—oooh, mysterious!) is gaining the loyalty of some twenty thousand jobless peasants. Reports describe Tony as having "hair down to his shoulders, a long tangled beard, an emaciated face, and a piercing eye," just like practically every other apocalyptic doomsayer this side of Zoroaster. He and the Counselees find a religious shantytown called Canudos, where they fuse Catholicism, native folk rituals, and witchcraft into a boiling stew of Last-Days obsession. Tony tells them to expect The End in 1900, and he and his piercing eye are fairly accurate on this one. Well, within three years, anyway. A host of Brazilian troops arrives in 1897 and annihilates the whole town.

NOVEMBER 13, 1900, RUSSIA:

A two-hundred-year-old Kargopol sect called the Brothers and Sisters of the Red Death—which, incidentally, would make a great name for a hardcore band—believes the world will end on this day. Suspecting that mass suicide will really give God the heavenly jollies, they decide to commemorate the occasion with a great big burnt sacrifice: themselves. Authorities in nearby St. Petersburg get wind of the plan and scramble to stop it. But where there's smoke, there's fire, and by the time the wagons arrive, one hundred brothers and/or sisters are already crispy. The survivors disband when the sun rises the next day without a hint of any sort of Red Death. There was already plenty of regular death to go around.

THE END IS NEAR, PART 2 (A TIMELINE: 1900 TO THE PRESENT)

You'd think there was plenty to keep us interested once calendars turned over to the twentieth century. Automobiles, motion pictures, radio, television, and computers came along. But so did evil dictators, world wars, the space age, nuclear proliferation, race riots, the Soviet Union, the Internet, that nice millennial number on the horizon—yeah, no wonder these are the years when apocalyptic fever volcanoed through the top of the thermometer. Here are some times when the fever spiked:

1908, PENNSYLVANIA:

At the impressionable age of twelve, young Lee T. Spangler experiences your basic trance-induced apocalyptic vision. Years later, as the owner of a grocery store in York, he seems to have suddenly remembered that revelation. So Lee steps up on a literal soap box in aisle five and informs his customers the world is down to its last can of beans. The whole enterprise is slated to end in October, he tells them, on account of a spectacular rein of fire. Many patrons believe. Others, troubled by the mere notion of a prophetic grocer, simply buy their sugar and flour and return home. October offers very little in the fiery doom department.

1914, OKLAHOMA:

Uh-oh. Our old friend Halley's Comet is back, packing chunks of doom amid the chunks of space dust and ice that form its wicked tail. A few entrepreneurs put a new twist on the usual Last Comet Standing nervousness, selling "comet pills" to protect the citizenry should the earth pass through its tail. And in Oklahoma, the members of a religious sect calling themselves the Select Followers have a great idea. We can appease the comet, they proclaim, by offering up a virgin sacrifice! Thankfully, they announce their intentions loud enough that the local law hears about it. The cops save the virgin, who really didn't have this in mind when she signed that True Love Waits pledge card.

It's also worth mentioning that 1914 is Charles Taze Russell's next big date o' doom. He churns this one out right after the spooky "Invisible Jesus" announcement of 1874. A few new calculations, and suddenly 1914 is unmistakably the year of Armageddon. So when World War I kicks off as the most horrific conflict the world has ever seen, the Jehovah's Witnesses have to work really hard to restrain their glee, what with all the death and everything. But the months keep passing, Jesus-free, until . . .

1915:

This is definitely the year, Russell announces. No question

1916:

Or this one! It's all a simple misunder—*thunk!* (Charles Taze Russell dies on Halloween in 1916.)

1918:

But right before his bucket gets kicky, Charlie sets yet another clock counting down to The End. But the only major end in 1918 is the November armistice that brings the war to a close. Which makes everyone in the world extremely happy, except the Jehovah's Witnesses. Because all the peace cramps their apocalyptic style.

1920:

J.F. Rutherford takes over for the Watchtower Society and starts revising history. His first step is to switch the arrival date of the reliable Can't-See-Me Christ. "1874? What are you talking about, 1874? Jesus returned to earth in 1914, just like Russell said. Yeah, that's right. You just can't see him. He's invisible. What? No, you haven't heard that anywhere before. Now go knock on some doors."

1925:

Rutherford says he expects Jesus to return this year, then starts immediately denying that he ever said it. At this point, the Pocket Guide speaks for all of us in saying: Shut up, Watchtower Society.

FEBRUARY 13, 1925, LONG ISLAND:

Ooooh, this is a good one. The Angel Gabriel appears to young Margaret Rowan in a vision. He tells Mags, who lives in L.A., that he's gonna go all Louis Armstrong up in the sky at the stroke of midnight on Friday the 13th (dun-dun-dunnnnnnnn!). Across the country, in Long Island, house painter Robert Reidt hears about Rowan's vision and gets excited about the impending trumpet blast. How excited? So much that he depletes his life savings to buy a billboard announcing a hilltop picnic and Rapture get-together. Bring a casserole! Lots of folks show up at the appointed time and place. The clock chimes midnight, and in unison, the faithful raise trembling hands and start chanting for Gabriel. A few agonizing minutes later, it's suggested that, hey, wait a second, maybe Margaret meant midnight *Pacific* time. Seeing how she lives in L.A. and everything. So they wait another three hours. At 3:00 a.m., more chanting. At 3:05, more disappointment. Everyone goes home, except for Robert, who has to clean up all the trash from the picnic.

1936, AMERICA:

Herbert W. Armstrong, founder of the Worldwide Church of God, tells his church that The End is very nigh. He's chock-full of other good ideas, too. One of them is the racially sensitive notion that, when the Bible refers to "the Jews," it doesn't mean the real Jews, but modern-day Christians like those in Herb's church. In fact, only those in his church will be saved. Yay! Anyway, he expects the gloominess of the Depression to hook up with the threat of war, and the resulting offspring is the "Day of the Lord." No such luck, though, so Armstrong takes it back and says he really meant 1975. Which, apparently, can sometimes be confused with 1936.

1938, U.S. EAST COAST:

Orson Welles broadcasts the Mercury Theater's production of *War of the Worlds*, interrupting a pretend radio show with breathless pretend updates about nothing less than a pretend invasion of earth by terrifying Martian forces. The program also contains a goodly sum of "this is only a dramatization"-type disclaimers, but no one hears those due to the mass hysteria. The next day, Welles feels bad enough to tell everyone he's sorry for scaring their gullible pants off.[1]

1947, BOSTON:

Way back in 1889, a dentist named John Ballou Newbrough predicts the destruction of all nations and onset of all-purpose anarchy, scheduled to begin promptly in 1947. That's not all, though. It seems the good doctor is quite gifted in ESP, which gives him a real distinct feeling he needs to buy this new invention called a typewriter. He does, and sitting at it early one morning, Newbrough watches as his hands just start typing as if independent from his body. The resulting masterpiece is a manuscript called the Oahspe Bible, which Newbrough believes to have been dictated to him by angels. Naturally, a cult springs up around him, and though they eventually come to the understanding that their founder is an unmitigated wack-job, there are still some devout Oahspeians active today. Because spiritual messengers can still communicate to us through wack-jobs. Kids, I think we've just learned a very valuable lesson.

1948, THE MIDDLE EAST:

The Jewish State of Israel is established in Palestine, a key event in the apocalyptic timeline detailed in Revelation. Christian fundamentalists get all wound-up, citing a couple of passages in the

---

1. Similar chaos reigned in Santiago, Chile, in 1944, and Quito, Ecuador, in 1949, when the Spanish versions of the play were broadcast.

Gospels that state the restoration of Israel must occur before Jesus comes again. And once that prerequisite has been met? According to the Bible, "this generation" will be the one with front-row seats to the Big Show. But how long is a generation? Forty years? Fifty years? One hundred years? Is it the entire generation of mankind? Everyone's still arguing about it a little more than a generation later.

1949:

Two days after President Harry Truman announces the first Soviet atomic test, a promising young preacher named Billy Graham declares we've got just another year or two left until Jesus comes back. He goes on to become a highly respected evangelist and influential friend to presidents, so apparently no one holds this failed bout of date-setting against him.

DECEMBER 21, 1954, AMERICAN MIDWEST:

Dorothy Martin (a.k.a. Marian Keech) cooks up a rabid UFO cult called Brotherhood of the Seven Rays (a.k.a. The Seekers). She mixes up a little clunky science fiction, Christian mysticism, and overt paranoia with her own channeled messages from the Boys Upstairs. And the message? Flood's a-comin', but if all seven of you Rays meet at the specified rendezvous point, we'll pick you up in the mother ship. Look for a giant glowing Frisbee. Said flying disc never arrives.[2]

APRIL 16-23, 1957, CALIFORNIA:

The Watchtower publishes the ramblings of a certain JW pastor named Mihran Ask, who predicts, yet again, the end of the world as the Jehovah's Witnesses know it. Sigh.

---

2. Leon Festinger wrote a groundbreaking book on the weird case of *The Seekers*. Called *When Prophecy Fails*, it studies cognitive dissonance and the effect failed prophecy has on "true believers." Which, evidently, is little or none at all.

APRIL 22, 1959, WACO, TEXAS:

Who knew the Branch Davidians had such history? A bug-eyed offshoot of the Seventh-Day Adventists, founded in the 1930s by no less than a Bulgarian washing machine salesman named Victor Houteff, the Davidians stash themselves away into a compound amid seventy-seven acres in sleepy east Texas. By April 22, 1959, they expect to be slaughtered, resurrected, and slurped right up into heaven via God's holy straw. Hundreds of the faithful gather for the big butchering . . . but no blood, no annihilation, no resurrection. The group is so disappointed it takes years before they perk up again in the '90s . . . thanks to a charismatic new leader named David Koresh.

FEBRUARY 4, 1962:

Take one quintuplified planetary alignment. Sprinkle in an always-mystifying solar eclipse. Stir in a potload of craziness—prayer vigils in Bombay, shelter-stocking in the United States, jittery sky-gazing everywhere—and you've got yourself an all-out Apocalypse Watch. Nothing happens, of course. But the Antichrist was born the next day, at least according to noted psychic Jeane Dixon.

1965-1966:

Not to be left out, Nation of Islam founder Elijah Mohammed takes a stab at end-of-the-world prophecy. Never a huge fan of The Man, Elijah's version of The End predicts white Americans being wiped out in a bloody apocalyptic battle, thereby reducing Caucasians to a sniveling underclass. At which point, black Americans, under the tutelage of the Nation of Islam, will rule. The years in question end up being big ones in terms of Civil Rights, but an all-out race war? Not so much.

1967:

Here comes the kingdom of heaven, according to the Reverend Sun Myung Moon, master and commander of the Korea-based Unification Church. And give him props for predicting a shiny, happy millennium, complete with a spiritual awakening. Which is always preferable to floods, fires, chaos, and out-and-out bloodshed. Good or bad, though, nothing happens. Why? Well, according to Mr. Moonie, it's because we're just not quite ready for enlightenment. But we are ready, however, for mass weddings.

Meanwhile, more apocalyptomania ensues as Israeli forces capture all of Jerusalem in the Six Day War. According to a literal reading of the New Testament, this meets another important biblical prerequisite, so everyone gets plenty excited about the completion of Leg 2 in the Rapture Relay. Leg 3 is the rebuilding of the Temple and the resumption of animal sacrifices there. Yippee! And yuck!

1969, CALIFORNIA:

Underappreciated rock 'n' roller Charles Manson perfects his weird blend of hippie-fied white supremacy and foists it on his own personal cult following, who call themselves "The Family." He's convinced The End is just around the block, right on the heels of a massive race war. So Chuck and his followers do what any normal, schizophrenic American with a Messiah complex and a Beatles obsession would do—they start killing people and blaming it on blacks. Members of The Family end up murdering eight people at the home of actress Sharon Tate (including Tate, who is eight months pregnant at the time). Manson goes to prison, where he's been putting the delusional Messiah act on freakish display ever since. The Pocket Guide would close this entry with something funny, but . . . sheesh.

1970:

A former Campus Crusade for Christ recruiter named Hal Lindsey publishes the runaway bestseller, *The Late Great Planet Earth*—in terms of popularity, the *Left Behind* of the '70s—which details his premillennialist vision for the End of Days. It's the first wildly successful book to compare current events to biblical prophecy, "it won't be long now" being the general theme. Three decades later, we're still waiting on the lateness and greatness. But almost single-handedly, Hal creates the doomsday/prophecy industry we know and love today, which makes books like the Pocket Guide possible. So good job, Hal. Gold star.

1974, INDIANA:

A fellow named Charles Meade informs the sleepy town of Daleville, Indiana, that the return of Christ will occur in his lifetime. Meade's credentials? Well, according to his résumé, he's been to heaven and seen God. You can't really argue with that. So Meade cranks up a little congregation in his garage, dubbing it "End Time Ministries." Before long, ETM is a bona-fide cult with a unique perspective on the final Apocalypse. Flood? Fires? UFOs? Nope. According to Charles, it's sticky white goo. We'll all be coated in a latter rain of, well, something like transparent mayonnaise. And that's the vaguely Freudian end. Blech. Meade is still at it today (which, technically, keeps his prophecy from being discarded into the "failed" bin), living in the Southwood Acres subdivision of sunny Lake City, Florida, where he's surrounded by a thousand or so followers who march lockstep to his bizarre teachings. These include an embargo on all media (books, radio, and television are tools of the devil), a ban on crying (it's a sin to lose your joy), and an absolute prohibition against having pets (as animals can harbor demons). And doctors? Stay away from them, too, because God heals without medicine. Meade and his followers rank pretty high on the freakiness scale, and they practically run Lake City. Just a note of caution next time you're in the area.

1975:

A big year for the Apocalypse. First in line are our old friends the Jehovah's Witnesses. You think the Potential Second Coming of 1914 was big? 1975 is bigger. Current president John Knorr gets infatuated with old Bishop Ussher and, citing the six thousandth year since Adam's creation, declares this year will definitely see the Big One.[3] The War of Armageddon approacheth, and God's got a mass genocide in the works that will kill the earth's entire population—Jews, Christians, Muslims, Maori Tribesmen, everyone. Well, everyone but active members of Jehovah's Witnesses who are good and holy and current on their dues. Devout JWs commence selling their homes, quitting their jobs, neglecting their houseplants, etc. When calendars turn over to 1976, however, they've had enough. They wing on from the religion in a major departure, leaving only the deluded leadership behind. Who promptly get to work on the next prediction.

Next in line is Charles Taylor, who is to doomsday prophecy what Stephen King is to novel writing. Which is to say, prolific. He gets his first big break onto the playing field this year, checking his doomsday calendar and seeing "Rapture Occurs" right there in bold print on Rosh Hashanah, the Jewish New Year. Soon, Rosh Hashanah is in the rearview mirror, Rapture-free. But Chuck's a real trooper, and he gets right back in the prophecy game, rescheduling The End for 1976. And 1980, 1982, 1983, 1985, 1986, 1987, 1988, and 1989. But who's counting?

---

3. Not to be confused with the official Watchtower Society's other end-of-the-world predictions in 1874, 1914, 1915, 1918, 1920, 1925, and 1941, which definitely did not see the Big One. Or even a Medium One.

1977:

Prolific author-of-Apocalypse Salem Kirban writes a book called *Countdown to Rapture*. In it, he predicts the future fulfillment of none other than the ninth chapter of Revelation. This passage is a real doozy, as it predicts swarms of locust assassins who have bodies like armed horses, faces like humans, and stingers like scorpions. Not to mention the long flowing hair of a woman and teeth like a lion. And wings, too, which allow them to fly around torturing people. (And to think some folks have trouble understanding the book of Revelation!) Anyway, Kirban believes these "assassins" refer to a swarm of killer bees that are, at this very moment, making a frantic, um, beeline toward the United States. So watch out. Nothing happens, but that doesn't keep Kirban from a tidy career peddling cornball prophecies, End-Times novels, and crackpot diet tips.

1978, GUYANA:

The Reverend Jim Jones introduces his brainwashed followers—and the world—to the dangers of Kool-Aid in the most unsettling Apocalypse/cult tragedy to date. Jones starts the People's Temple as an urban mission in Indianapolis back in the 1950s, focused on good things like racial harmony and social justice and meeting the needs of the poor. But somehow, along the way, it morphs into a very bad thing: a major doomsday cult. By the mid-'70s, Jones has developed a mongo Messiah complex and a legion of followers. Invigorated by a combustible mix of paranoia and End-Times speculation (Jones expects a racial holocaust and nuclear Armageddon to destroy the U.S. any minute)—plus a handful of negative exposés of their weirdness, including child abuse—members of the People's Temple hit the road, fleeing to Jimmy's personal four-thousand-acre colony in Guyana, aptly named "Jonestown," in 1977. There, the needle on the nuts-o-meter really starts to jump.

Jones has a pretty substantial drug habit by this time, feeding his paranoia, monomania, and messianic tendencies all at once. He sets up loudspeakers and rants at his followers night and day. He subjects them to hard labor (kids included), beatings, shock torture, and sexual abuse. He even forces them to take part in "suicide drills," should a self-imposed Apocalypse ever become necessary. Eventually, word of the disturbing goings-on reaches the States, and Congressman Leo Ryan of San Francisco makes a trip to personally investigate, along with a crew of photographers and journalists. Long story short, the investigators eventually figure out that life there sucks. But as they prepare to leave (along with a handful of defectors), armed People's Temple security guards step out of the jungle and open fire. Ryan dies, along with a few others. One plane escapes to get help.

Knowing what lies ahead, Jones fires up the loudspeakers one last time and calls the flock together for a special group refreshment break. On the menu is a deadly concoction of Kool-Aid and cyanide. Most take it willingly, dying facedown, arm-in-arm. The few who protest are forcibly injected with the poison or shot. A grand total of 638 adults and 276 children die. Jones and his family are among them. And forevermore, the mere idea of a doomsday cult gives people the heebie-jeebies.

1980, WASHINGTON, D.C.:

Backed by strong support from the Moral Majority (founded by *Left Behind*'s Tim LaHaye), Ronald Reagan is elected president of the United States. His administration is considered a successful one for a variety of reasons, but foremost for our purposes is the fact that his staff was perhaps the most Apocalypse-minded in history.

Examples? In 1981, James Watt, Reagan's Secretary of the Interior, testifies in a Congressional hearing about his plans for the use of our national resources and public lands. His strategy fails to impress—at all—because it leans heavily on no less than the imminent Rapture and Tribulation. Says Watt: "I don't know how many future generations we can count on until the Lord returns." In other words, let's drill, pollute, and otherwise destroy, because soon it'll be an apocalyptic wasteland anyway. Yeesh. That same year, Secretary of Defense Caspar Weinberger offers his opinion on international events: "I have read the Book of Revelation and, yes, I believe the world is going to end—by an act of God, I hope—but every day I think time is running out . . ."

And Mr. Reagan himself? Seems he was on the same page as Watt and Weinberger. It's one thing to be a lunatic fronting a harmless UFO cult. But it's quite another when there's a red phone in your Oval Office with nuclear holocaust on speed dial. And when you're tagging your primary foe with a cute nickname like "The Evil Empire"? Scary.

DECEMBER 21, 1981:

Remember our good friend Hal Lindsey of *The Late, Great Planet Earth*? According to that worthy tome, this date is his expected Rapture-rama. The math is easy: Take the re-establishment of Israel in 1948, which we all know officially kicked the End Times into high gear, and add forty years. Popular theory—among rapturous Revelationophiles, at least—holds that forty years equals a generation. And since The End is only a generation away from that starting point, we can pinpoint earth's Last Day for 1988. Subtract a seven-year tribulation, and you've got yourself a 1981 Rapture.

Or not. In fact, forget we even mentioned it. Circa January 1, 1982, Hal changes some stuff, grabs a calendar, and starts setting a bunch more dates. Though they consider him generally apostate, the Watchtower Society nods in approval.

1982:

Ye olde catastrophic planetary alignments. Back in 1974, otherwise respectable astrophysicists John Gribben and Stephen Plagemann get jiggy with a theory called the "Jupiter Effect," which they introduce in a book of the same name. They postulate that the alignment of all nine planets—Jupiter included—on the same side of the sun in 1982 could result in all sorts of gravitational complications. These include solar flares, planetary wobbling, radio interruptions, weather fluctuations, tectonic indigestion, massive earthquakes, and jittery squirrels. And guess what? It happens. Well, at least the anticipated planetary alignment part. But all the devastation and turmoil? Nope.[4]

1982:

"I guarantee you," televangelist and future presidential candidate Pat Robertson says in a May 1980 broadcast of *The 700 Club*, "by the end of 1982 there is going to be a judgment on the world." He forecasts a Russian invasion of Israel, which will domino into a nuclear Armageddon, which will result in the deaths of two billion people. Unfortunately, the Soviet Union refuses to cooperate with Mr. Robertson and his ironclad guarantee.[5]

1985:

Lester Sumrall, a Pentecostal preacher, publishes a quaint little book called *I Predict 1985*. First and foremost of those predictions is the end

4. Turns out Gribben and Plagemann were just playing a fun game of scientific "what if" and felt a little sheepish about all the attention. Gribben even refuted the book's conclusions. But no one cared, especially those, like Hal Lindsey, who used the theory to back up their predictions.
5. Bonus, unrelated note: Robertson claims to have altered the path of hurricanes through prayer. Why isn't this guy working for FEMA?

of the world. When January 1986 rolls around, Lester works on his New Year's resolutions. First and foremost on the list is a new book.[6]

APRIL 29, 1987:

Dr. Leland Jensen, establisher of the Bahá'í faith and apparently the fulfillment of every prophecy of every religion ever (or so he tells us), predicts the earth will soon tow Halley's Comet into its rip-roaring orbit. Said comet will pelt our petunias with frozen comet pellets and other nasty debris. Earthquakes, tidal waves, and sundry annoyances are expected to result, and on April 29, the comet itself will crash-land in our collective driveway, leaving a path of widespread destruction. Or, perhaps, not. The widespread destruction is a no-show, and soon after, Leland pulls a page right out of the Jehovah's Witnesses handbook. In an inspired bit of sidestepping, he announces, "Wait, something *did* hit the earth, but you couldn't see it because it was *spiritual*." Riiiiiiiiight.

AUGUST 16 & 17, 1987:

Everybody say hello to the Great Harmonic Convergence. Author, artist, educator, and Earth Day founder José Argüelles stages a huge weekend party to prevent the earth from slipping out of its, ahem, "time beam," sending the entire Marble spinning out into space. Which would have been a bummer. So José orchestrates an international psychic pep rally to occur simultaneously at sacred places across the globe, for the purpose of cleansing the planet's history-stained karma. According to his calculations, enough people concentrating intently on the business at hand will help keep the earth in orbit and, better yet, unwrap a New Age, chock-full of peace, love, and harmony. And guess what? We're still here, so . . . thanks, psychics.

6. The new book hits shelves in 1987, creatively titled *I Predict 2000 A.D.*

1988:

Speaking of psychics, Austrian-born spiritualist Alfred Schmielewski is a super one. In fact, it says so on his business card: Maha Yogi A.S. Narayana, Canada's World Renowned Super Psychic. "Lord Narayana" pays the bills by giving readings at state fairs and the like, claiming to be the world's foremost authority in the field of world prophecy. So when he predicts that the greatest natural disaster the planet would ever see would strike Montreal in 1988, people listen. Okay, not really. Despite his lofty title, Alfred is a pretty sorry psychic. He proves it in 1999 when he answers the door at his home only to be shot in the head by an unknown assailant. Guess he didn't see *that* coming.

SEPTEMBER 11-13, 1988:

Also in 1988, Israel turns forty. Based on the trusty a-generation-is-forty-years belief, fundies the world over chew their nails in anticipation of the big day, making 1988 a banner year for Second Coming scenarios. One of the biggest is a neat little booklet written by NASA scientist Edgar C. Whisenant. Called *88 Reasons Why the Rapture Could Be in 1988*, it pegs the Great Uplift for Rosh Hashanah, and sells an astounding 4 million copies. And because he is a NASA scientist—and nothing ever goes wrong at NASA—dude is completely convinced his space math has nailed The End. "Only if the Bible is in error am I wrong, and I say that unequivocally," he says. Unequivocally! Everyone believes him, including the levelheaded folks at Trinity Broadcasting Network, who suspend regular programming to screen "Help! Everyone's Been Raptured But Me!" instructional videos for non-believers.

SEPTEMBER 15, 1988:

Either Whisenant's Bible or his NASA math fails when nothing happens September 11–13. So he recalculates and finds some sort of mistake (surprise!) and announces that the Rapture is now slated for 10:55 a.m. on September 15. Don't be late.

OCTOBER 3, 1988:

Okay, Edgar's having some serious doubts by now, unequivocally, but he trudges through and gamely pushes the date back yet again . . .

1989:

. . . at which point he just gives up on 1988 and writes another book: *The Final Shout: Rapture Report 1989*. Everyone now: Shut up, NASA scientist.

APRIL 23, 1990:

Messenger Elizabeth Clare Prophet (a.k.a. Guru Ma), leader of a survivalist/doomsday/militia cult called the Church Universal and Triumphant, predicts a nuclear holocaust on this date, followed by a good dozen years of outright mayhem. So she instructs her thousands of followers—who practice a grab-bag of Christian mysticism, occult spiritualism, Eastern philosophy, and major appreciation of the Second Amendment—to sell their property and join her in a sizable bomb shelter in Montana to await The End. Unfortunately, her insistence that the shelter be stocked with crateloads of military weaponry results in the arrest and conviction of many cult members (her husband included) on federal weapons charges. April 23 passes without any sort of nuclear activity. At least, not the world-destroying kind.[7]

---

7. You know Christopher Paolini, the homeschooled Montana kid whose runaway fantasy bestseller *Eragon* hit all the big lists in 2004? His parents met as members of the Church Universal and Triumphant, but left in 1987 before all the shelter-building hoopla.

1991:

Lots of Armageddon enthusiasts giggle contentedly when the Gulf War breaks out, including none other than Nation of Islam leader Louis Farrakhan. Remember Elijah Mohammed's race war predictions in 1965? King Louie carries on in the footsteps of his forbear, describing the burning oil fields and violence as the fulfillment of Scriptures, and no less than the War to End All Wars. But it's not. In fact, it's not even the War to End All Wars Between a President Named George Bush and an Evil Dictator Named Saddam Hussein.

1992:

Way back in the '70s, Lori Adaile Toye is your basic farm wife and mom to three small children. Leave it to the "Ascended Masters" to shake things up. One night, out on the farm, four white-robed beings step holy foot into Lori's dreams, where they stumble around in the dark until one of them locates the prophecy/nutcase light. They flick it on. In a series of dreams, the Four spill the details on a major update to earth's geography. One of the highlights involves a rearrangement of the American coastline by a meteorite. California pretty much disappears. Which, according to Lori, should bring about a global spiritual awakening. Because spiritual enlightenment will be the first priority for tourists should Las Vegas suddenly become a beach town.

OCTOBER 28, 1992, KOREA:

Prophecy meets puberty when twelve-year-old Bang-Ik Ha of the Korean Tami Church declares Jesus Christ himself has been whispering sweet somethings in his ear. Those somethings include his plans for an October 28 Rapture. Turns out young Ha is only one of many prophets brought into the spotlight by a certain Lee Jang Rim, a bestselling doom-and-gloominary within the Korean Christian community. Rim's faith is, to put it mildly, extreme. In it, true believers can look forward to a glorious Rapture. Everyone else? Death, dismemberment, and wide-ranging horror. And believing ain't enough in itself. You've gotta be waaaaay over the top in your willingness to suffer for your faith. Which gives us tales of Rim's followers having abortions so they won't be too heavy to lift into heaven, and of one's faith being measured by the amount of blood he or she can cough up during fits of raving supplication. Bang-Ick, indeed! But then the date passes, and Lee Jang Rim gets sent up the river for duping his followers out of at least $4 million. Even better: That cool four-mil? Invested in bonds set to mature in 1995. Sweet.

1993:

Faith healer and slayer-in-the-Spirit Benny Hinn says the Rapture is nigh, so get ready. Except for you homosexuals. You're not going anywhere until 1995, when God will personally destroy you. Go away, Benny.

APRIL 19, 1993, WACO:

The Apocalypse-minded Branch Davidians are back, this time under the leadership of a messianic charmer and rock-star wannabe named David Koresh. A former Seventh-Day Adventist, like most of his followers, Koresh had fixed the date of Armageddon for 1995. But events in the spring of 1993 cause him to push the timetable up. In late February, an ATF team shows up at the Davidians' Waco compound with a search-and-arrest warrant. They're after Dave for stockpiling weapons and abusing children (he's unquestionably guilty of both). A gun battle ensues, killing four federal agents and six cult members, and wounding twenty others. Next comes a fifty-one-day standoff, which culminates in a catastrophic self-imposed fire, apparently set as U.S. tanks tear through the compound's walls, firing tear gas canisters. The blaze kills seventy-five Davidians, including twenty-one children. The FBI and Department of Justice are soundly criticized for their decision-making during the standoff, especially for not seeming to fully grasp the destructive bent of Koresh's End-Times obsession. As for the remaining Davidians? They're still stubbornly awaiting the Apocalypse.

JULY 25, 1994:

In the summer of 1993, "Sister" Marie Gabriel Paprocski—we use quotation marks because her sistership is self-appointed—starts spreading the news that a killer comet will strike Jupiter on or before July 25, destroying the earth in, like, the biggest cosmic explosion ever. She buys full-page ads in major newspapers warning everyone to shape up. And whaddya know? The sister is right. Sort of. There is a significant comet strike on Jupiter in 1994, occurring July 16. It's worth mentioning, however, that astronomer Brian Marsden had also made a little prediction a couple months earlier—that Comet Shoemaker-Levy 9 was on a direct collision course with the Big Jupe. So . . . very impressive soothsaying there, sister. Or rather, "sister."

DECEMBER 17, 1996:

Little Sheldon's idyllic childhood is similar to that of most other kids from Buffalo: playing Cowboys and Indians, reading sci-fi magazines, receiving extraterrestrial visitations, and attending learning conferences aboard spacecraft. The usual stuff. Little Sheldon from Buffalo grows up to become famous psychic Sheldon

Nidle, a "representative" and lecturer with the Galactic Federation of Light. In that capacity, he goes all Hollywood with his End-Times vision, promising the general themes of destruction and chaos at the hand of 15.5 million X-Wing Fighters winging toward earth (and guided by a squadron of angels). Strangely enough, earthlings fail to notice said millions of spacecraft on the selected date. But that's to be expected, Sheldon explains to us silly earthlings. Because all his predictions are spot on—destruction of the world via atomic death ray included—and what we're experiencing now is just a big holographic projection. We've been bamboozled!

1997, TOKYO:

Remember the deadly Sarin gas attacks on the Tokyo subway system back in the mid-'90s? Those are the responsibility of one deranged, blind pseudo-messiah named Shoko Asahara, of the Aum Shinrikyo cult, who mixes in a little bioterrorism with his trail mix of Eastern spirituality, Revelation-obsession, and love of all things Nostradamic. So when he gets the feeling that The End has a paying fare aboard Bus '97— lugging with it the twin suitcases of biological and nuclear warfare—he decides to make sure the job is done right. In addition to the subway attacks, which kill nineteen people, Aum cultists spray the U.S. Embassy with botulism bacteria, and pelt additional government buildings with a host of other nasties and toxins (the strains are, fortunately, not strong enough to kill anyone). Plans for a nerve gas attack on U.S. soil are also in the works, until the authorities capture the cult leader and toss his blind Asahara into prison. This doesn't deter the Aum cult, though. They still worship the guy as a living Christ and regard his jail cell as sacred ground, dutifully waiting for his instructions regarding the next Apocalypse.

MARCH 26, 1997:

Failed opera singer Marshall Herff Applewhite and his soul-mate, a spirit-channeling registered nurse named Bonnie Lu Nettles, hook up in the 1970s and start their own little saucer cult. Typical story: He's a two-thousand-year-old alien, she's no less than God Almighty, and the mother ship is supposed to swing by to pick them up in 1975. It . . . doesn't. Bonnie ends up being mortal after all and dies of cancer in 1985. Applewhite (known to his followers as "Do," as in "Re Mi Fa So") continues to attract cult members, collecting them in a sprawling house in Rancho Santa Fe, California, under the pleasant moniker "Heaven's Gate." Most of them are computer geeks. They build websites. They shave their heads. They wear colorful little jumpers and matching tennis shoes. And the guys get castrated.

They all live happy little productive robot-like lives until 1997, when amateur astronomer Chuck Shramek mistakes a star for a "Saturn-like object" following the Hale-Bopp Comet. Shramek goes on the Art Bell radio show, and before you know it, his "object" has become a bona-fide UFO hiding in the comet's wake. Which is good news for Do and his androids, because that's exactly what they've been waiting for all this time. It's Bonnie Lu! She's swinging by to pick us up! So the Gaters shoot a creepy video in which they each say bye-bye to family and friends. After dropping the tapes in the mail, they share a few spoonfuls of poisoned applesauce. Police get a tip from a family member who gets nervous after watching the "I'm-leaving-on-a-spaceship" video. Next stop is the nightly news, complete with footage of each member stretched out dead on his or her cot—their shed "earthly vehicles" covered by a purple cloth.

OCTOBER 1997, ST. LOUIS:

Pentecostal pastor Kenneth Hagin predicts Christ's Second Coming and the Rapture of the saints, starting in St. Louis, "the heart and center of the nation." Of course. Never having personally been to St. Louis, the Pocket Guide can't give an accurate report. Did anything happen? Is anyone still there? Did Jesus become mayor or what?

1998:

Take the number of the Beast (666) and multiply it by the Trinity (3) and you get none other than 1998. Since Jesus is obviously some sort of clever math trickster, this must be the year he returns for the sequel. This according to a book called *Ominous Portents of the Parousia of Christ*, by Henry R. Hall. Ominous, indeed.

MARCH 31, 1998, GARLAND, TEXAS:

Hon-Ming Chen, top dog of God's Salvation Church (otherwise known as Chen Tau, "The True Way"), claims Jehovah is jetting toward earth via a spaceship due to arrive at 10:00 a.m. on this date. And a few days prior, he's slated to make an appearance on every single television set in the U.S. On channel 18, to be precise. Chen brings his minions to Garland (near Dallas) to await The End. Why? Because the name sounds kind of like "God Land." No, seriously.

JULY 1999:

Doomsday according to Nostradamus. Perhaps you're familiar with his work. Born in the sixteenth century, Nostradamus was a French physician and astrologer and all-around mystic. He's primarily remembered for a ton of cryptic four-line poems/prophecies he composed while having visions of the future. His supporters credit him with accurately predicting the death of King Henry II, the reign of Charles de Gaulle, the rise of Adolf Hitler, the mysterious demise of Pope John Paul I, and the baffling popularity of Ashlee Simpson. Except for the part about Ashlee Simpson. One of the most notable predictions concerns the present year:

The year 1999, seven months,
From the sky will come a great King of Terror:
To bring back to life the great King of the Mongols,
Before and after Mars to reign by good luck.

In other words, July 1999 promises some sort of sky-is-falling scenario involving "the King of Terror"—could be nuclear bombs, or killer hailstones, or a plague of asteroids, or a parachuting Stephen King—coupled with the resurrection of the "great King of the Mongols." The Antichrist, maybe? Genghis Khan? Anyway, July passes with very little terror and hardly any Mongol sightings. Except in Mongolia, where they say that sort of thing is quite common.

AUGUST 6, 1999:

The Branch Davidians are back in the news, as a few of their surviving members have a gut feeling this is the day their former leader, David Koresh, will rise from the grave and judge the world, 2,300 days after his death (as per Daniel 8:14, a verse about the rebuilding of "the Temple"). Still waiting.

AUGUST 11-18, 1999:

This is a scary week, featuring no less than 1) the last total solar eclipse of the millennium; 2) the Perseid meteor shower; 3) a fly-by of NASA's plutonium-loaded Cassini space probe; 4) the Grand Cross planetary formation (don't ask); and 5) the presence of Comet Lee in the neighborhood of our solar system. Some suspect Nostradamus may have had all these portents in mind, as this is still July according to the ancient Julian calendar.[8]

And on the 18th? Well, this is the day the Amazing Criswell, a bestselling "prophet" from the 1960s, foretold The End in amusingly descriptive fashion. This from *Criswell Predicts: From Now to the Year 2000*: "The world as we know it will cease to exist . . . on August 18, 1999 . . . And if you and I meet each other on the street that fateful day . . . and we chat about what we will do on the morrow, we will open our mouths to speak and no words will come out, for we have no future." Just now the Pocket Guide's author tried to type something sarcastic, but his fingers would not move. What can that mean?

2000:

Aaaaaaaand here we go. Seriously, if the Pocket Guide were to list all the end-of-the-world predictions that started piling up regarding Y2K, you'd probably still be reading when The End *does* arrive. Suffice it to say, the loonies are out in full force even before everyone gets worked up about the Y2K Bug. Our old pal Hal Lindsey's at it again. So are fundamentalist Mormons, who pull their kids out of school and look to the sky for the lowering of the New Jerusalem onto Independence, Missouri. Christian fundies like Pat Robertson and Jerry Falwell suspect Bill Clinton will gloss himself Mega-Dictator for Life and rule with a pasty fist. And everyone from Sir Isaac Newton to Martin Luther to Jonathan Edwards to a Native American spiritual leader named Sun Bear imagine something related to The End—be it the Rapture, the launch of the

8. There's a thirteen-day gap between the Gregorian calendar we know and love and the Julian calendar Nostradamus would have known and loved.

thousand-year reign, the Last Judgment, or planetary Apocalypse—will be greenlighted on January 1, 2000. Happy New Year, everyone!

JANUARY 2, 2000:

Crap.

2000:

Back in 1997, journalist Michael Drosnin writes a bestselling book called *The Bible Code*. It claims that the Hebrew Bible contains a very complex word-searchy code—based on equidistant letter sequences arrayed in a huge matrix, if you must know—that predicts events that come to pass thousands of years later. With the help of a computer scanning the grid, he's able to connect, for instance, the words "Dallas" with "President Kennedy." Everyone gets a little creeped out by it, especially when a few decide the messages were put in the Scriptures by God himself (encryption being a favorite pastime of the Heavenly Father). And one of those messages? World War III is calendared in for 2000. Unfortunately, most scientists and stat geeks say the random "hidden message" sequences Drosnin gets so jazzed about can be produced in almost any text. Even this one. Expect the hair-raising *Pocket Guide Code* to hit stores in 2006.

2000:

A step above the Watchtower Society in terms of apocalypticizing—and that's really saying something—is that checkout line staple and bastion of truth-telling, the *Weekly World News*. So far we've been able to steer clear of its special blend of self-assured and freaky doomsday predictions, but this one is just too much. Seems the WWN gets its hand on the prized "Bethlehem

Scrolls," ancient prophecies written by the original three wise men. Who knew? In the year 2000, these scrolls attest, Billy Graham will die a torturous death at the hands of terrorists, Pope John Paul II will be zapped by a personal pontiffied nuclear device, and Jesus Christ—who, apparently is back in the neighborhood—gets mowed down by evil National Guardsmen (controlled by the UN, of course) wielding automatic weaponry. Zoiks!

SEPTEMBER 11, 2001: NEW YORK CITY

Funny, isn't it, how no one is able to predict this day, probably one of the most significant and tragic in American history? It has all the makings of an apocalyptic event—thousands of deaths, a billion-dollar economic impact, early rumbles of war—yet the only prophecy about it is a made-up one purportedly from Nostradamus, and later proven to have been a hoax.

Wait—never mind. Not so funny after all.

MARCH 24, 2002: HOLLYWOOD

Orthodox Christian Paul Smirnov emails a number of media and religious groups with a good-news-and-bad-news message. The good news is that this year's March 24 Oscar telecast will be shorter than usual. The bad news is that the brevity will be due to an asteroid that will strike the Kodak Theatre that very night, annihilating Hollywood and its demon-spawn residents. The prophecy is based on a creative interpretation of Revelation 18:21-23, in which Hollywood producers are the sorcerers, Los Angeles is Babylon, and newcomer Paul Smirnov plays the role of the Fruit Loop.

2003:

According to the Hindu calendar, Sree Vishiva Karma Veera Narayana Murthy, avatar of Krishna, will arrive on earth to personally usher in a 108-year reign of grooviness and good tidings (and hopefully, name shortenings).[9] Of course, the appearance of SVKVNM will be preceded by a number of bad tidings, including bloody rain, incurable diseases, the circulation of coins of dubious quality, and the emergence of male goats with, um, milkable teats. Rain of blood and cheap coinage we can deal with, but lactating goats? Shiver.

2004:

Buoyed by the popularity of Volume One of *The Bible Code*, Mike Drosnin brushes up on his crossword skills and looks for more random spookiness in the Good Book in *The Bible Code II: The Countdown* (dramatize much?). He's not disappointed, as the trusty "code" reveals we're in the Last Days. Most spooky is a prediction and/or "message from God" that bio-chemical and nuclear attacks against New York City and Jerusalem will usher in World War III. The result will be nothing less than the elimination of all human life. Hey, wait a second. Wasn't WW3 the plan for 2000? Bible Code guy? Shut. Up.

OCTOBER 17, 2004:

Spend a lot of time with the dimensions of Noah's Ark, as personally dictated to Old Noah in Genesis, and they'll eventually reveal to you when to expect the milky mammaries of The End! So says Clay Cantrell, who starts calculating all the cubits and ends up with a timetable for the Second Coming. God sighs. Lately, it seems, we've been cracking his secret codes like walnuts.

---

9. Technically this entry shouldn't be here, because "the end of the world" is a concept foreign to Hinduism, which views time as cyclical rather than linear. Therefore, no beginning and no end. But the thing with the goats is just too good to pass up.

It only seems like the end of the world for tourists and villagers near the Indian Ocean in the aftermath of a devastating tsunami. The day after Christmas, hundreds of thousands are swept to their deaths in India, Indonesia, Sri Lanka, Thailand and elsewhere. Beaches are washed away. Entire villages are wiped out. It's an international tragedy of apocalyptic proportions. If only Mr. Cantrell and the Ark had warned us about *this*.

KNOW YOUR POTENTIAL ANTICHRISTS
(A GALLERY OF CANDIDATES)

Since the earliest parts of the New Testament were written and disseminated across the ancient Middle East, the people of the region—and the citizens of the larger world around them— have been patiently awaiting the arrival of one of history's most famous and influential leaders, an earth-changer who will make his presence known in grand fashion right before the end of the world.

The Antichrist.

What, you thought we were talking about the Son of God? Nope. Sorry. Jesus is a known entity. We've met him before. We've read about him for years. Faithful believers already have personal relationships with him. He brings good news, but at this point, he's just not that newsworthy.

But the Antichrist? Now that guy's captivating. All we have on him is a generic name. A few descriptions. A prediction or two. Some downright scary prophecies. As much as Christ is known, the Antichrist is unknown. That's why the Pocket Guide, along with everyone from fundamentalist doomsayers to authors of End-Times fiction to pop culture aficionados is intrigued by the answer to the third most popular barstool question ever: Who Might Be the Antichrist?[1]

Besides, what good is an apocalyptic good–versus–evil battle without all the evil?

After surveying a dizzying collection of crap produced by conspiracy theorists, wild-eyed Christian apocalypsochists,[2] eschatological scholars, and all-around end-of-the-world enthusiasts, we have developed an official list of prerequisites that must be met by any world leader vying for the position of Antichrist. After discussing the criteria, we'll then survey those prominent figures who, past or future, have been finger-pointed as likely candidates for the post.

Following, then, are the ten basic requirements for the job:

---

1. The second most popular barstool question ever: *Is (fill in the blank) a sport?* The most popular barstool question ever: *In a fight between (blank) and (blank), who would win?* (Note: These ratings not based on any real research.)
2. Not an actual word.

10 REQUIREMENTS FOR THE ANTICHRIST

❶ A MAN

The Antichrist must be male, according to Revelation 13:18, which encourages believers to figure out what 666 means, "for it is the number of a man." That's pretty clear, unless the use of "man" is generic—like "human"—to distinguish from, say, a walrus Antichrist. But that would be silly. Antichrist = male. Sorry, ladies.

❷ AN ENEMY OF GOD

Which is pretty obvious, considering the name and everything.

❸ AUTHORITY AND/OR POPULARITY

The Beast is described as having "ten horns and seven heads, with ten crowns upon its horns," which is bizarro, even as metaphor. Some believe the heads and crowns mean the Antichrist will rule ten countries. At any rate, he'll pretty much do what he wants during his short-lived reign, uniting the world under his slick leadership. And world domination? Requires more than a few followers.

❹ A PEACEMAKER

Many premillennialists believe a false, temporary peace will rule during the Last Days, possibly in the form of a treaty in the Middle East. "Swords into ploughshares" and so on. But the Antichrist will eventually break the treaty, beginning a reign of terror.

❺ FALSE MESSIAH/WORSHIPABILITY

At some point, the Antichrist will convince the Jews he is their Messiah, the true Christ. He'll declare himself divine, and all the nations of the world will worship him (Revelation 13:8).

❻ DEADLY HEAD WOUND

The Beast in Revelation 13 is described as having a head "wounded beyond recovery," until it suddenly becomes healed, resulting in an outbreak of awe and wonder.

❼ 666/MARK OF THE BEAST

Another obvious one.

❽ JEWISHNESS

Popular apocalyptic theory holds that the Antichrist must be a Jew or have a close connection to the Jews. Not that the Bible says much about it, but sure, why not? Because if history has shown us anything, it's that anti-Semitism is harmless.

❾ NEW ROMAN EMPIRE/ EUROPEAN CONNECTION

Many think a "revived Roman empire"—by which they usually mean the European Union or some sort of New World Order—will be given power for a short time under the control of the Antichrist.

❿ OTHER AREAS OF SUSPICION

This is the final catchall category to contain the whole stew of conspiracy theories and other gristly leftovers.

A final note before we get started. Most speculation on the Antichrist comes not necessarily from the Bible, but from popular apocalyptic theory espoused by your Hal Lindseys, Pat Robertsons, and Tim LaHayes of the world (and those are the level-headed ones). They contend, of course, that their Antichrist speculation is biblical, but what they've really got is a composite figure drawn from a bunch of vague prophecies and metaphorical descriptions.[3] So who knows? Revelation doesn't even actually use the word *antichrist*, which should tell you something right there. It's basically a stinky pile of nail-biting, conspiracy-theorizing, and loosely xenophobic/anti-Semitic conjecture. But it's fun, so let's get crankin'.

THE ROMAN EMPEROR NERO

Lived: First century A.D.

Claim to fame: Fifth and last emperor of the Julio-Claudian dynasty. Great-grandson to Marcus Aurelius. Known primarily for being a torturer of Christians, an emperor of ill repute, and a dude who fiddled while his city burned to the ground (though, curiously, the violin had not yet been invented).

1) A Man. Yes, though not a very good one.

2) Enemy of God. By all means. Got his jollies by persecuting the Christians of Ancient Rome. Favorite methods included

3. Not that you'll ever look this up, but here is where most of the Scripture-based Antichrist speculation comes from: the "Prince who is to come" (Dan. 9:26; 7:7-8, 19-26; 8:23-25); the "abomination of desolation" (Matt. 24:15, Dan. 9:27); the "man of lawlessness" (2 Thess. 2:3); the few passages in the Bible where the actual term "antichrist" is used (1 John 2:18, 22; 4:3; 2 John 7); and the descriptions of "The Beast" in Revelation 13 and beyond.

crucifixion, human torches, and sewing folks up in animal skins to be torn apart by wild dogs. Cruel *and* unusual.

3) Authority/Popularity. Yes on the power. No on the popularity. Nero's reign was rocked by scandal and paranoia. His citizens hated him, and his list of enemies seemed to double every month. As did his weight, but that's another story.

4) Peacemaker. Gained a few meager brownie points for rebuilding the city of Rome after its Great Fire. Of course, it's suspected that he started the fire in the first place, to allow him the privilege of reconstructing the city to greatness—and basking in the acclaim. Which rhymes with "lame."

5) False Messiah/Worshipability. The Emperor of Rome, during those days, was increasingly seen as being not only an agent of the gods, but a god himself, guaranteeing life and fulfillment to his followers. Nero is said to have wanted to give Rome a new name: "Neropolis." Also, he killed Christians who refused to bow to him, which generally leads to the appearance of universal worship, if not the real McCoy.

6) Head Wound. Close. With the help of his secretary, Epaphroditus, Nero committed suicide by stabbing himself in the throat.

7) 666/Mark of the Beast. The Greek *Neron Kaiser*, translated into Hebrew, adds up to a numerical value of 666. Nero was also referred to as a "beast" by historians of the period.

8) Jewishness. Not personally, but Nero's wife (and former mistress) Poppaea Sabina was Jewish, and the persecution of the early Church was supposedly a result of her urgings.

9) New Roman Empire/European Connection. No, but the connection to the Ancient Roman Empire is pretty solid.

10) Other Reasons for Suspicion. In addition to his Jewish wife, Nero was also influenced by a legendarily Jewish "inner circle," which may or may not have had something to do with the Great Fire. Also very into a broad spectrum of religions, including Zoroastrianism, a handful of virgin-mother goddess cults, and the mystical Gnostic stylings of the magician Simon Magus.

Could Nero be the Antichrist? Possibly. A decent candidate, and an all-around bad guy who murdered his parents, his brother, his pregnant wife, and a slew of other family members. The very definition of a bloody tyrant and enemy of God, which is why Preterists—those who believe the events in Revelation were fulfilled in the first century—are fully on-board the Nero-was-Antichrist train. They're joined by a number of early Christian authorities who believed John was writing to first century Christians about events that were to take place right around the corner.[4]

THE POPE (ANY POPE)

Lived: First century A.D. to present

Claim to fame: The Bishop of Rome and worldwide head of the Roman Catholic Church. Throughout history, just about

---

4. This assumes, however, that Revelation was written before the destruction of Jerusalem in 70 A.D., rather than toward the end of the first century, as many scholars believe. Otherwise, Nero would have been dead by the time John had the dream. Which is, like, the easiest kind of prophecy.

every pope has been tagged with the Antichrist label, especially by evangelical anti-Catholic fundamentalists, who won't let go of the crazy idea that the Vatican is the Whore of Babylon as described in Revelation 17–18.

1) **A Man.** Yes. The papacy is still an exclusive boys' club.

2) **Enemy of God.** This one's a stretch, although some popes have been naughtier than others. Like Alexander VI in the late 1400s, who bribed his way into the position and soiled his pointy white hat with nepotism, greed, murder, and the occasional orgy.

3) **Authority/Popularity.** Lots. As leader of the largest church in the world and the absolute monarch of Vatican City, the pope wields considerable political and moral power. Before 1870, he also had authority over a large chunk of territory in Central Italy called the Patrimony of St. Peter. And he's been appointed to his position by God, so who's to argue?

4) **Peacemaker.** Let's get specific. John Paul II was engaged in Middle Eastern diplomacy for several years, working tirelessly to sooth Palestinian-Jewish relations, to promote reconciliation between Catholics and Jews (see "Jewishness" below), and even to bridge the gap between Muslims, Jews, and Christians. Which really, really bothered those who looked at his interfaith dialogues and saw the first steps toward a one-world religion based around the Church of Rome.[4.1]

5) False Messiah/Worshipability. You know how the pope comes out on the balcony of the massive Basilica of St. Peter and waves to the teeming crowds of supplicants and admirers below? And they all seem to cheer and weep and carry on like he's a spiritual rock star? That also really, really bothers some people. And the pope's claim to be "Vicar of Christ" on earth is also suspect, because *vicar* comes from the Latin root *vicarius*, which literally means "substituting for, or in place of." And a guy claiming to be a substitute for the Son of God? Yep. Pretty fishy.

6) Head Wound. In 1981, John Paul II was shot in the stomach and nearly killed by a Turkish gunman as the pope entered St. Peter's Square via Popemobile (an assassination attempt that some say was the partial fulfillment of a prophecy made decades earlier by Padre Pio, the famous stigmatic). He recovered just fine, though—which raised eyebrows among the fanatical set, who went to work trying to figure out how "head wound" could be interpreted symbolically as a reference to the stomach.

7) 666/Mark of the Beast. Back in the second century, Irenaeus proposed that the ancient Greek word *Latienos* ("Latin-speaking man"), using the numeric equivalents of Greek letters, added up to 666. It also works with *Italika Ekklesia* ("Italian Church"). And the

---

4.1 This edition of the Pocket Guide had the misfortune of being printed between the passing of John Paul II and the naming of his successor. It is unclear at this point whether the new pope will be a leading candidate for the Antichrist. But odds are good. Odds are *always* good.

Latin *Vicarius Filii Dei* ("Vicar of the Son of God") that's said to be inscribed on the papal tiara. Truly the pope must be the Antichrist. If only we could figure out which pope.

8) **Jewishness.** Nope. Sorry. Even though John Paul II, who grew up amid a flourishing Jewish culture in Poland, was perhaps the most pro-Jewish pope in history. He was the first pope ever to visit the Synagogue of Rome and made pit stops at Jerusalem's Wailing Wall during his frequent visits to the Holy Land.

9) **New Roman Empire/European Connection.** Who needs a New Roman Empire when you're the head dude right in the middle of the place where the Old Roman Empire had its heyday?

10) **Other Reasons for Suspicion.** Revelation 17 says that the seven heads of The Beast represent the seven hills of the city where the Great Harlot (The "Whore of Babylon") lives. Quick: Name a city famous for its seven hills. That's right! Rome! You win a gold star![5] Or, better yet, a microchip implanted in your forehead.

So could the pope—or a pope—be the Antichrist? Probably not, despite the long-standing Protestant tradition of equating the two. In fact, it's more popular these days to tag the pope as the False Prophet, the powerful, authoritative guy who tells everyone to pony up and start bowing to the Antichrist. That takes a fair amount of influence, especially if you're suggesting that people worship, for instance, Prince Charles (see page 101).

5. Of course, Rio de Janeiro has seven hills, too. But does the Pope live in Rio?

ADOLF HITLER

Lived: 1889 to 1945

Claim to fame: One of the most significant leaders in the history of the world (but not in a good way) as Führer of Nazi Germany. His racial policies resulted in the deaths of millions and the destruction of Europe during World War II.

1) A Man. Yes.

2) Enemy of God. Duh. Hitler!

3) Authority/Popularity. A gifted public speaker and author of the popular *Mein Kampf* ("My Struggle"), a screed detailing his political plans for Germany and ideas on race. *Time* magazine's "Man of the Year" for orchestrating the Munich Agreement in 1938. Oops.

4) Peacemaker. Despite being considered a candidate for the Nobel Peace Prize in 1938 (yep, the Munich Agreement), not so much. Those who opposed him as Führer were visited by the Gestapo and eventually disappeared in concentration camps. Had many of his enemies killed during the "Night of the Long Knives" in June 1934.

5) False Messiah/ Worshipability. Thanks to the Nazi propaganda machine, most Germans saw Hitler as their own mustachioed personal savior who protected them from the Depression, from the Communists, from the pesky Allied powers, and from, of course, the Jews.

6) Head Wound. Killed himself in his Berlin bunker with a bullet to the head.

7) 666/Mark of the Beast. If a=100, b=101, and c=102 (and so on), then add up the values of "HITLER" and you get 666. Chilling!

8) Jewishness. Speculation holds that he may have had a partially Jewish ancestry. Regardless, Hitler was completely anti-Semitic. He once stated his goal was to eradicate the Jewish race (along with Communism) from the face of the earth.

9) New Roman Empire/European Connection. Matches up pretty nicely with the Third Reich, which followed the Second Reich (the German Empire from 1871-1918) and the First Reich (The "Holy Roman Empire of the German Nation," tenth century to 1806).

10) Other Reasons for Suspicion. Born on Easter in Austria's Braunau am Inn, the polar coordinates of which are 48.25 N, 13.05 E. And what's the cosine of 48.25? None other than .666![6] Also said to have had hypnotic eyes.

Could Hitler have been the Antichrist? Nah. Unlikely. Back in the 1940s, some expected a resurrection following his suicide—

6. For all you math geeks out there, this assumes the Earth's radius to be 1.

and a number of conspiracy theories have the most powerfully evil man of the twentieth century still alive and, oh, tending bar in Argentina or something, despite being way past the century mark—but that's about it. Hitler was the personification of evil and everything, but probably not the Antichrist.

JOHN F. KENNEDY

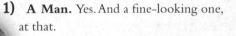

Lived: 1917–1963

Claim to fame: The thirty-fifth president of the United States, and the first Catholic elected to the Oval Office. He is primarily known for preventing nuclear war during the Cuban Missile Crisis and for his conspiracy-rich assassination in Dallas, Texas, on November 22, 1963.

1) A Man. Yes. And a fine-looking one, at that.

2) Enemy of God. Depends what you believe about Catholics. Once Kennedy was elected, he became the most famous (and powerful) Catholic in the world, even more so than the pope. To the Roman-Catholic-Church-is-the-Whore-of-Babylon contingent, these were nail-biting circumstances indeed.

3) Authority/Popularity. Kennedy was probably the most popular U.S. president in history. The Catholic connection was a big deal, and he was admired by millions of the U.S. faithful. Young women loved him, too, because he was, well, strappingly handsome and stuff. In fact, Kennedy and his wife, Jackie, were embraced the world over for their charisma and youthful vigor. Their days in the White House posthumously became known as "Camelot"—a brief, shining moment of grace and optimism before tragedy.

4) Peacemaker. Kennedy's role during the Cuban Missile Crisis can't be denied. Many historians believe this was the closest the world ever came to nuclear war, and it was Kennedy's resolute thinking and political skill that kept the situation under control.

5) False Messiah/Worshipability. Many believed Kennedy would turn into the pope's lackey during his presidency, making an alliance with the Vatican to form a supreme religion/government centered around him and Rome.

6) Head Wound. This one's a gimme. Kennedy was killed with a shot to the head by Lee Harvey Oswald in possibly the most famous and controversial assassination in history. Conspiracy theories abound, but the graphic nature of Kennedy's "head wound" was too much for the apocalyptic to ignore. Even today, many are waiting for him to return from the grave dressed in his world-domination suit, with Henry Kissinger as his False Prophet. No, really.

7) 666/Mark of the Beast. Kennedy received 666 votes at the 1956 Democratic Convention, narrowly losing the vice presidential nomination to Estes Kefauver. That's right: *the* Estes Kefauver.[7]

8) Jewishness. No. But Jack Ruby—the man who shot and killed Lee Harvey Oswald before he could formally be charged for the murder—was Jewish. Aha!

9) New Roman Empire/European Connection. See above about the fear that the nation's first Catholic president would team up with the Vatican to rule the world. Just like it was often suspected that Ronald Reagan, the nation's first Hollywood president, would team up with the Screen Actors Guild to rule the world.

10) Other Reasons for Suspicion. Kennedy's supposedly innocent "Camelot" connection to the Arthurian legend is suspect to many, because the mythical King Arthur suffered a mortal head wound by the sword, was carted off to the mystical Isle of Avalon to rest in peace and/or be healed, and was expected to return in glory at some point and rule over Great Britain. Just like Kennedy evidently plans to do when he miraculously returns as the head-wound-healed Antichrist.

So could John F. Kennedy be the Antichrist? It's conceivable. He's not the worst candidate by any means. Being dead, of course, kinks up the plan considerably, though a return from the grave could go a long way toward winning over potential worshipers, including non-Catholics. Plus, wouldn't we all like someone to clear up that grassy knoll theory once and for all?

---

7. No, the Pocket Guide hasn't heard of him, either.

RONALD REAGAN

Lived: 1911–2004

Claim to fame: The two-term fortieth president of the United States and former governor of California, known for actively confronting Soviet aggression during the Cold War and implementing policies that eventually led to the downfall of Communism. And also for liking jellybeans.

1) A Man. Yes.

2) Enemy of God. Not really. Though a product of Hollywood and an irregular churchgoer, Reagan was much-beloved by conservative evangelicals of the Religious Right. Which, according to some, is reason enough to be wary.

3) Authority/Popularity. Tons. Practically the father of the modern conservative party, he energized Republicans and appealed to a good many traditional Democrats, too. Reagan's folksy good humor and positive outlook earned him the nickname "The Great Communicator."

4) Peacemaker. Credited by many with winning the Cold War, and known for labeling the Soviet Union as the "Evil Empire." Also remembered for challenging Mikhail Gorbachev to "tear down this wall" when speaking in front of the

Berlin Wall in 1987. By the end of 1989, the wall was gone, followed by the eventual collapse of the U.S.S.R. and the end of the Cold War.

5) False Messiah/Worshipability. Hmmm. Well, Republicans really liked him.

6) Head Wound. Shot in the chest in 1981, only a few months into his presidency, by John Hinckley, Jr. In fact, the bullet barely missed his heart. Reagan's Press Secretary, James Brady, suffered a serious head wound in the assassination attempt, which left him partially paralyzed. So no head wound for Reagan, but a very serious one for his spokesman. Later, a few also argued that the Alzheimer's disease Reagan battled in his twilight years could also be considered a metaphoric "wound" to the head—and from which he could miraculously recover and rule the world. But, honestly, that's just tacky.

7) 666/Mark of the Beast. Ronald Wilson Reagan: three names, six letters each. There's your 666. Plus, when the president and Nancy retired, they lived in a Bel Air mansion given to them by wealthy friends. Its address? 666 St. Cloud Road. Nancy had the number changed to 668.

8) Jewishness. Not ethnically. But in 1985, in an address given at the Air Force base in Bitburg, West Germany, Reagan speechified the following: "Twenty-two years ago, President John F. Kennedy went to the Berlin Wall and proclaimed that he, too, was a Berliner. Well, today freedom-loving people around the world must say, I am a Berliner, I am a Jew in a world still threatened by anti-Semitism, I am an Afghan, and I am a prisoner of the Gulag . . ." A bold-faced confession!

9) New Roman Empire/European Connection. Reagan's vice president and eventual successor, George H.W. Bush, was (and still may be) a major proponent of the New World Order. Plus, Nancy used to consult her astrologer before finalizing the president's schedule—and the practice of astrology is one of the few surviving remnants of the ancient faith of Babylon.

10) Other Reasons for Suspicion. On election day in 1980—when Reagan was voted into office—the winning lottery number in both Maryland and New Jersey was 666. In 1984, on the Saturday after his reelection, Maryland's winning lottery number was, again, 666. Also, if you rearrange the letters of Ronald Wilson Reagan, you can get the anagram "Insane Anglo Warlord." Which, if you ask the Pocket Guide,[8] is stone-cold proof right there.

So could Ronald Reagan be the Antichrist? Please. He was just a charismatic politician and well-liked U.S. president whose leadership at the end of the Cold War inspired many. But to label him the Antichrist because of a few dumb coincidences? That's insane. Which is probably why you get eight thousand hits when you Google "Ronald Reagan Antichrist."

MIKHAIL GORBACHEV

Lived: 1931 to present

Claim to fame: Leader of the Soviet Union from 1985 to 1991, whose attempted reforms helped lead to the end of the Cold War.

1) A Man. Yes.

---

8. If you rearrange the letters of Pocket Guide, you can get a similarly spooky anagram: Pig-Toe Ducke.

2) Enemy of God. Yes. Communist dictator who rose to power amid an atheistic, godless empire. (It's a well-known fact that God is a capitalist.)

3) Authority/Popularity. A popular and well-respected statesman during his reign, at least in the West (though Russians don't like him much, since his reforms led to the collapse of their country). *Time* magazine's "Man of the Decade" for the 1980s.

4) Peacemaker. Was awarded the Nobel Peace Prize in 1990 for helping end the Cold War.

5) False Messiah/Worshipability. Once, in a television interview, compared himself to Jesus Christ—who was falsely condemned by his own people—when asked to explain his lack of respect in Russia.

6) Head Wound. Dude, check out that birthmark. Looks like a freakin' blood stain!

7) 666/Mark of the Beast. The numerological equivalent of "Mikhail S. Gorbachev" in Cyrillic computes to 1,332, which is twice the Mark of the Beast. Also, that splotch on his forehead? He takes it very seriously. In fact, he had it trademarked in early 2004 to prevent a Russian vodka company from putting it on its labels. That's right: He's got a trademarked birthmark.

8) Jewishness. Not in terms of ethnicity, but the Gorbster did gradually loose restrictions on Russian Jews and their practice of religion after coming to power. And millions of Jews emigrated from Russia to the U.S. or Israel after the collapse of the U.S.S.R. So he's practically *meshpucha*.[9]

9) New Roman Empire/European Connection. A member of the Club of Rome, a German-based global think tank comprised of the world's leading politicians, scientists, economists, and the like. Which, to conspiracy theorists, is just a roundabout way of saying "New World Order."

10) Other Reasons for Suspicion. One of the major sponsors of the Earth Charter in the late 1990s, a sixteen-point secular document thought by some to be a proposed replacement for the Ten Commandments and the foundation of a new worldwide religion to replace Christianity.

Could Gorby be the Antichrist? Yes. An excellent candidate. He may be Public Enemy number one among the Apocalypse-minded for as long as he sticks around.

9. Yiddish for "extended family."

SADDAM HUSSEIN

Lived: 1937 to present

Claim to fame: President and ruthless dictator of Iraq from 1979 to 2003, at which point he was deposed (and later captured) by the United States and its allies. Currently being tried for war crimes, which include the mass murder and torture of millions of Iraqis.

1) **A Man.** Yes. And check out that virile mustache!

2) **Enemy of God.** Yes. According to some prophecy buffs, Saddam thinks of himself as a reincarnation of Nebuchadnezzar, the great king of ancient Babylon who destroyed the nation of Israel in sixth century B.C., enslaving God's chosen people in the process.

3) **Authority/ Popularity.** Because of his defiance of the United States, considered a hero by many in the Arab world.

95

4)   Peacemaker. Um, no.

5)   False Messiah/Worshipability. See Nebuchadnezzar stuff above. Some of his followers, even today, believe Saddam is immortal. Propaganda can be effective.

6)   Head Wound. Nope, unless you're talking a figurative head wound, which the U.S. soundly delivered to Baghdad during the war.

7)   666/Mark of the Beast. Born April 28, 1937, Saddam was captured on December 13, 2003. Which made him, at the time of his capture, 66.6 years old!

8)   Jewishness. Not Jewish. In fact, an enemy of the Jews, on account of his lifelong support of the Palestinians and his nervous habit of occasionally lobbing missiles toward Jerusalem.

9)   New Roman Empire/European Connection. Not only does Saddam think of himself as a modern-day Nebuchadnezzar, but word on the prophetic street was that he was rebuilding the ancient city of Babylon—the ruins of which are located in Iraq— brick by brick. So maybe when Revelation 18 talks about Babylon, it's not the New World Order or the Vatican or the United States, but actually, you know, Babylon.

10)   Other Reasons for Suspicion. In the famous Mabus/Third Antichrist prophecy from Nostradamus ("Mabus will soon die, then will come, / a horrible undoing of people and animals"), some intuit that "Mabus" is Saddam. How? By using the anagram game of reverse lettering. "Mabus" becomes "Sudam," which is really, really close to "Saddam." So watch out, people and animals.

Could Saddam be the Antichrist? A couple of years ago, yeah. But after the whole spider hole scenario and capture by U.S. troops, his candidacy for The Beast has lost a little steam. We'll have to wait and see, of course, but odds are he's not the one. And as long as we're on the subject, he's probably not the second coming of King Nebuchadnezzar, either.

WILLIAM JEFFERSON ("BILL") CLINTON

Lived: 1946 to present

Claim to fame: The two-term forty-second president of the United States and former governor of Arkansas, known for becoming only the second president to be impeached following his affair with saucy White House intern Monica Lewinsky. The Senate acquitted him, though, and he left the office with one of the highest approval ratings ever for a retiring U.S. president.

1) **A Man.** Yep. Acts like one, too.

2) **Enemy of God.** This one's a stretch, as Clinton has been a practicing Southern Baptist, a student of the Bible, and a professing Christian for most of his life. His wife, Senator Hillary Rodham Clinton, is a Methodist.

97

He went to Georgetown, a Catholic university. Dude's got religion all over him. But many Christians don't like him due to his moral failings and his advocacy of abortion and the fact that he's a liberal and, well, the possibility that he's the Antichrist. Enemy of God, though? Naw.

3) Authority/Popularity. Huge. A saxophone-playing, Big Mac-eating, womanizing good ol' boy, Clinton was embraced during his two terms despite the scandals that tainted his administration. As a public figure, he maintains a high profile in contemporary politics and world affairs. His autobiography, *My Life* (released in the summer of 2004), set worldwide sales records, including first-day sales of 400,000 copies. In comparison, Ronald Reagan's post-presidency memoirs (*An American Life*) sold 20,000 units in its first week.

4) Peacemaker. Clinton took office in January of 1993. Within a month, his Secretary of State, Warren Christopher, was trucking around the Middle East trying to stir up the stagnated Israel/Palestine peace process. Not too long after, Bill acted as the master of ceremonies at the signing of the Oslo Accords, a peace agreement negotiated between the Israeli government and the Palestine Liberation Organization. (The famous photograph of the 1993 signing shows Clinton with his arms stretched out, bridge-like, between Yitzhak Rabin and the late Yasser Arafat.) In 2000, ex-President Clinton convened a summit at Camp David between Arafat and Israeli Prime Minister Ehud Barak to keep the peace process in motion. In fact, Clinton has vowed to see the resolution of the Israeli-Palestinian conflict in his lifetime. And he wants to be right in the thick of it. Which is nice of him, but also a little Antichrist-y.

5) False Messiah/Worshipability. He's pasty as a plucked chicken, but in a 1998 *New Yorker* essay, author Toni Morrison once famously called Clinton "our first black president." He came from an impoverished background, yet he tickled the collective fancy of affluent soccer moms. He was a Rhodes scholar with the nickname "Bubba." He lied from the Oval Office about as often as he quoted the Bible. Then there was all that talk about how he "felt our pain." This guy has a little something for everybody. Which is a key trait when you're recruiting worshipers.

6) Head Wound. Some have suggested that, in Clinton's case, the head wound is metaphoric: the Lewinsky scandal. The tawdry affair was thought to have been the death of his presidency. After being impeached, Clinton was on the verge of being forced out of office . . . until he miraculously recovered from "the fatal wound." The Senate acquitted him, and he ended up retiring from office with astronomical approval ratings. Aaaaaand that's about as far as we want to go thematically relating the phrase "head wound" to Monica Lewinsky. Because the next stop? Smutsville.

7) 666/Mark of the Beast. Using the traditional numerical values of corresponding letters in both Hebrew and Greek—the two languages of the Bible—"William J. Clinton" adds up to 666.

8) Jewishness. If he was the nation's first black president, couldn't he have been the first Jewish one as well?

9) New Roman Empire/European Connection. In 2004, the Brussels-based Union of Small and Medium-sized Enterprises awarded him the European SME Award for his presidential efforts to create a flourishing world economy and international foreign trade. Did we mention that Brussels is home to the headquarters of the European Union? Meanwhile, Clinton has kept close ties with NATO and the U.N.

10) **Other Reasons for Suspicion.** In May of 1998, Clinton signed the controversial Executive Order 13083, which attempted to assign mega-power over the states to himself and all federal agencies. It centralized all government powers (national, state, and local) into the federal government, rendering all other laws obsolete, and stated that the federal law "shall define the moral, political, and legal character of [Americans'] lives." Which meant what, exactly? That the government could control the social and religious behavior of its citizens? Interesting. Once everyone found out what Clinton had done, however, the ensuing public outcry led to the order's immediate suspension.

  So could Bill Clinton be the Antichrist? He's not in the White House anymore, but he's kept his foot wedged in the public door more than any other ex-president. He's still in great demand as a speaker, both nationally and worldwide. He's still a major player in U.S. politics. And he's still a deeply polarizing figure—people either love him unconditionally or don't trust a word he says. Could it be him? Definitely, his sincere Christian beliefs notwithstanding.

CHARLES PHILIP ARTHUR GEORGE MOUNTBATTEN-WINDSOR (THE PRINCE OF WALES)

Lived: 1948 to present

Claim to fame: Eldest son of Queen Elizabeth II and Prince Philip, Duke of Edinburgh, and heir apparent to the British throne. Also Duke of Cornwall, Earl of Chester, Baron of Renfrew, Lord of the Isles, and another dozen or so snooty titles that have little or no meaning today.

1) A Man. Yes.

2) Enemy of God. Disputable. Future head of the Church of England who is also said to have become enamored of the Orthodox faith, with a little Eastern mysticism tossed in for flavor. But, in any case, he seems to be on okay terms with the Almighty.

3) Authority/Popularity. Substantial. His popularity soared after he handled the death of Princess Diana—and his subsequent single-parenthood—with grace and dignity. Well-respected as a performer on the world stage, Charles has also become popular with many left-wing politicians and underprivileged citizens, thanks to his charity, The Prince's Trust. As for authority, there's the matter of him being next in line to become King of England. And he's rich as figgy pudding.

4) Peacemaker. A principal player in the signing of the 1993 Oslo Accords, a series of agreements negotiated between the Israeli government and the Palestine Liberation Organization (PLO).[10] And any time you combine "Mideast peace process" and "Israel" in the same sentence, you're bound to give End-Times crazies a good case of the shakes. In fact, many were convinced the Oslo Accords were the opening bell for the seven-year Tribulation. Until 2000, that is, when they realized Armageddon had either passed quietly or not at all.

5) False Messiah/Worshipability. He is credited for the success of the Rio Earth Summit and thus the Kyoto Protocol, and he has spearheaded the push for enforceable environmentalism worldwide. So, he could be the potential savior of the planet, environmentally speaking. And don't forget the House of David stuff (see "Jewishness" below).

6) Head Wound. Not yet, anyway.

7) 666/Mark of the Beast. Using the ancient Jewish numerological system called *Gematria*, "Prince Charles of Wales" computes to 666. Or, you know, whatever.

8) Jewishness. The College of Heralds in London has traced the royal lineage back to King David, which makes Prince Charles the 145th direct descendant of Israel's greatest king. Which is a pretty

---

10. If you define "principal player" this way: one of the heavies in the Oslo peace discussions—along with Yassir Arafat, King Hussein, and Yitzhak Rabin—was Lord Victor Mischon, Charles' personal attorney. For Antichrist watchers and conspiracy theorists, this is enough of a connection to make Charles no less than the fawning errand-boy of Satan himself.

impressive Jewish pedigree for an Anglican. Even more impressive is a family tree that spans three thousand years of history. Great googly-moogly.

9)   New Roman Empire/European Connection. Well, he's heir to the throne of Great Britain, which has to count for something. A major player within the European Union, too.

10)   Other Reasons for Suspicion. According to kooks on the Internet, Prince Charles is secretly one of the most powerful people in the world. He and twenty-four other individuals make up the top-secret Order of the Garter, which is the ruling force over the top-secreter Priory of Sion, the Knights Templar, the Rosicrucians, all the Freemasons in the world, and every other clandestine group no one has ever heard of despite the hard work of *Da Vinci Code* novelist Dan Brown, and who are probably at my door right now with meat hooks and antimatter guns to give me ye olde what-for because the Pocket Guide just spilled the beans. Anyway, Prince Charles is secretly the boss of all these guys, so heads-up.

11)   Yet Another Reason for Suspicion. The imagery on his coat of arms is practically riddled with End-Times graffiti. For instance, there's a red dragon (just like in Revelation 13!). There's also a beast that could be a leopard with a lion's mouth and bear's feet (just like in Revelation 13!). Or maybe it's just a badly drawn lion, because all British royalty are represented by lions. Just a hunch, though.

Could Prince Charles be the Antichrist? Well, if all the above stuff is true about him being the Chief Poobah of all covert societies everywhere, the originator and keeper of the surreptitious handshake, the designer of the Crackerjack® Decoder Ring, and the heir of the ancient King David of Israel, then he must be pretty influential. He must also be a great performer, because all this time he's seemed like such a flop-eared royal dope. I mean, carrying on an affair with Camilla Parker-Bowles when he was married to Lady Diana? Helloooooo!

Odds are good, though. Put him right up there with Gorby and Clinton.

WILLIAM HENRY (BILL) GATES III

Lived: 1955 to present

Claim to fame: Cofounder and current chairman of Microsoft, the world's largest software company and producer of the omnipresent Windows computer operating system. As of 2004, Bill Gates was the world's wealthiest man, with an estimated net worth close to $30 billion.

1) A Man. Yes. A very rich one.

2) Enemy of God.
Inconclusive. In a 1995 PBS interview with David Frost, Gates said, "In terms of doing things I take a fairly scientific approach to why

things happen and how they happen. I don't know if there's a God or not, but I think religious principles are quite valid." Not that being agnostic makes you an enemy of God, but it's probably safe to say they're not golfing buddies.

3) Authority/Popularity. Microsoft Windows is by far the most popular computer operating system in the world, monopolizing the desktop industry with a market share near 95 percent. Same goes for Microsoft's Internet Explorer in the browser wars. And Microsoft Office, when it comes to business applications. Microsoft is the eight-hundred-pound gorilla in the world of computing, and Gates is the gorilla master.

4) Peacemaker. Not exactly. In fact, lots of people hate Gates and his company because of Microsoft's ubiquity and power in the marketplace. In the late 1990s, the U.S. Department of Justice even brought a series of antitrust actions against them for anti-competitive and monopolistic practices, tarnishing Gates' innocent code-boy image. Other competitors don't like Microsoft for predatory pricing, alleged code swiping, incompatibility issues, and for being so stinking successful in general.

5) False Messiah/Worshipability. A few computer geeks worship the guy because, more than anyone else in history, he made dorkiness cool. But lots more computer geeks don't like him because he's all lame and corporate and Windows is not near as rad as open-source groundbreakers like Linux. Others are impressed that Gates intends to give most of his fortune away via the Bill & Melinda Gates Foundation (the world's largest charitable foundation, named after him and his wife), which focuses primarily on education and global heath issues, including Third World disease prevention and AIDS research.

6) Head Wound. No. **Bad haircut?** Yes.

7) 666/Mark of the Beast. By adding up the ASCII[11] values of "Bill Gates 3," you get 666. Same results for "Windows 95." And "MS-DOS 6.31." Plus, there's the whole implanted microchip theory relating to the Mark of the Beast, and who better to harness computers and technology for his malevolent purposes than the world's foremost computer guru?

8) Jewishness. Yes. A secular Jew, but a Jew all the same.

9) New Roman Empire/European Connection. Gates is said to have attended meetings of the ultra-powerful (and secret—shhhh!) Bilderberg Group. This invitation-only forum of international bigwigs meets annually to discuss globalization and related issues. And somehow during their meetings they find time to control the leadership of all major nations in the world—including the U.S., deciding who will be president and when—and evidently have been doing so since World War II (this according to breathless websites that favor multiple exclamation marks and liberal use of ALL CAPS!!!!!!!!!). Anyway, the Bilderberg Group is a favorite target of conspiracy theorists and New World Order/Illuminati watchers.[12]

10) Other Reasons for Suspicion. Bill and Melinda, through their foundation, are members of the Global Alliance for Vaccines and Immunization (GAVI), which oversees the administration of vaccines to children throughout the world. At least that's what

11. American Standard Code for Information Interchange, an old-school computer coding system based on the Roman alphabet and modern English.
12. It's worth noting that fellow candidates Mikhail Gorbachev, Bill Clinton, and Prince Charles have also been on the invitation list for Bilderberg meetings.

they say. Some believe they actually oversee the injection of tiny nanotransistors into the bodies of unsuspecting children who will eventually fall under Bill's malicious control, as part of his plan for world domination and wide-ranging evil.

So could Bill Gates be the Antichrist? The love of money, as they say, is the root of all evil. So the Pocket Guide wouldn't put it past the world's richest (and most powerful?) man to have some sort of devious scheme in place for the future. But does anyone really picture the Antichrist wearing glasses and a rumpled cardigan? Or Bill Gates leading a vast demonic army against Christ in the Battle of Armageddon? That's a tough one.

FUN WITH ESCHATOLOGY
(A PAINLESS INTRODUCTION TO APOCALYPTIC THEORY)

Unless you're faced with an approaching mega–comet or a plague of runaway nanobots (*see chapter 6*), the main focus of any end-of-the-world discussion is religion. Specifically Christianity, which takes its cues from the Bible. Which most Christians agree to be authoritative on any discussion of life, salvation, and the End of Days. Which would be exceedingly helpful if anyone could agree at all about what is actually being said in those discussions.

The Bible in general, and the New Testament in particular, is bursting with information about the Second Coming of Jesus Christ and the events that occur before and after it. Chapter 24 of Matthew hits it in great detail, with Jesus himself providing most of the commentary. Paul touches on it in 1 Thessalonians, with a few words about the Rapture. Then there's Revelation, which devotes eighteen chapters of ink to The End in bright, shiny Technicolor® trippiness. It's presented as an ecstatic vision the Apostle John experiences in exile on Patmos, and makes about as much sense as any run-of-the-mill hallucination and/or dream sequence.

But for all the bizarre detail Revelation sketches out regarding Christ's return, there's still a heap of confusion about what it all means. The whole apocalyptic enchilada is relentlessly metaphorical. It's stacked high with ambiguity, and that's why there are as many interpretations of these biblical passages—about the events they foretell, the people involved, the timing and sequence—as there are wide-eyed obsessives who write about them.

What's the result? Only the most fascinating and increasingly obscure branch of Christian theology ever: eschatology (es-KUH-tology), the study of the "end of things." It's no stretch to guess that more has been written on this topic than any other aspect of the Christian faith (particularly on that great equalizer, the World Wide Web), especially as it concerns major apocalyptic events like the Rapture, the Tribulation, the Millennium, and the Second Coming. A lot of this stuff is alarmist, racist, xenophobic drivel. Ground-level support of these theories can be intense. Some theological camps are so passionate about their version of the Apocalypse that they're convinced that anyone believing otherwise is the proud owner of a one-way cruise to the fiery pit, with the Angel of Darkness at the helm.

All the more reason we ought to have some idea what they're so obsessed about, right? What follows, then, is an analysis of the five major systems of End Times theology among Christians.[1] A few of these terms we mentioned briefly in the Apocalyptionary (*chapter 1*). But you were just aching for more detail, right?

Thought so.

SYSTEM 1:
HISTORICAL PREMILLENNIALISM

Most Premillennialists—your Hal Lindseys and Tim LaHayes and the like—will boast that their system is the way all good Christians have believed from the time Jesus was tramping around in the first century. That's true. Sort of. But not completely.

Back in the early centuries of Christianity, being a Christian wasn't very fun. Persecution by Roman authorities was all the rage, and thus many Christians lived in constant fear of, say, being captured and fed, limb-by-limb, to a snarling pack of wild dogs. Which can really screw up your weekend. So hope for a better world was a major drawing point of the faith, and the eschatology of the day reflected that hope. Early Christians got a lot of comfort out of Revelation, reading it with the understanding that Jesus would show up any day now and mop the floor of the Coliseum with their Roman enemies. The victorious Christ would turn the tide, intervening in history, overcoming evil with good, and ushering in a new age of peace.

The early Church Fathers were definitely premillennialists and interpreted the Scriptures literally as prophetic descriptions of future events. According to their timeline, the Antichrist shows up and ushers in the seven-year Tribulation. When the closing bell rings on

---

1. Primarily Protestants, as Catholics don't get near as worked up over the End Times. For the record, most Catholics are amillennialist, though they probably wouldn't call it that.

the Big Trib, Jesus returns and conquers the forces of evil. He then rules, in a visible kingdom, with the faithful (who have shed their earthly bodies and are now sporting spiritual ones) for a thousand years of peace and happiness. After the temporary millennium comes the final judgment. Moaning, groaning, gnashing of teeth. And after that? Then you get an eternity of peace and happiness with Jesus on a new earth, which will be similar to heaven. But not exactly similar. Because, you know, it's on earth.

The primary difference between historical premill and modern-day dispensational premillennialism is the timing of the Rapture. The old guys have it occurring after the Tribulation. The new guys think God'll yank us out of here before the bad stuff begins.

Anyway, with the help of Emperor Constantine, Christianity eventually became the official religion of Rome in the fourth century. So no one worried anymore about being torn apart by lions. It looked like the Christian cause was going to stick, and maybe peace and happiness would pop up on their own without Christ's physical help. That's one reason historical premillennialism gradually fell out of favor. Which is a nice way to say it was condemned as heresy at the Council of Ephesus in 431.[2]

WHO BELIEVED THIS STUFF? Almost all the early Church Fathers were on board with historical premillennialism. Some names you might recognize are Irenaeus (who was a disciple of Polycarp, who was a disciple of John—yep, that John), Justin Martyr, Tertullian, Hippolytus, Commodianus, and Lactanitus. But, then, maybe not. As for contemporary notables, you've got George Eldon Ladd, John Warwick Montgomery, and J. Barton Payne. You probably haven't heard of them either.

WHAT'S THE BEST PART ABOUT IT? Jesus comes back and rights all the wrongs of our trib-and-trouble world.

---

2. The changeover was quick. Led by Augustine, church leaders shifted from a foundational belief in premillennialism to an amillennialist bent over the course of a few decades. They condemned premill belief in a literal, future 1,000-year reign as superstitious and unorthodox. And because most premillennialists tended to rely heavily on Revelation for their beliefs, many early Church leaders were hesitant at first to accept the book as Scripture.

WHAT'S THE WORST PART? No Rapture. You first have to trudge through the trib-and-trouble before you get to any of the good stuff.

SYSTEM 2:
DISPENSATIONAL PREMILLENNIALISM

The heresy is back and better than ever. Undeterred by the fact that premillennialism was officially condemned in ancient times—and was later viewed warily by Protestant Reformers like Martin Luther—it gets resurrected in 1830 by John Nelson Darby, an Irish Anglican minister and originator of the Plymouth Brethren movement. Darby proposes a system called dispensationalism, which breaks the Bible down into seven separate time periods, or dispensations, during each of which God deals with his creation through different covenants. (For instance, God had a different kind of relationship with Adam, tra-la-la-ing amid the innocence of the Garden, than he did with mankind after the Ten Commandments were made known to Moses. And because of the sacrificial death of Jesus Christ, God has different principles for dealing with men today under the covenant of grace. Which you should be thankful for, because otherwise you'd still be sacrificing animals every few weeks to stay on good terms with the Almighty).

Darby is credited with introducing the concept to the States when he arrived in 1862, but it didn't really hit the big-time until the publication of the Scofield Reference Bible in 1909 by Cyrus Ingerson Scofield, a recovered alcoholic with no formal theological training. The Scofield was one of those brick-thick Scriptures with copious notes in the margins, going into detail about the meaning and application of the verses you're supposed to be reading. In the case of the Scofield, these notes carried the perspective of a strident dispensationalist. So, before long, serious Bible readers of the early twentieth century had dived headlong into the premill pool. Scofield had talked them into it. Because who can argue with something that's right there in the Bible? Even if they're "notes" and not actual Scripture?[3]

What you really need to know about dispensationalism is that it is now the predominant view among modern evangelicals. Its adherents believe very strongly (and literally) in the millennial kingdom. Like historical premillennialism, it holds that a seven-year period of Tribulation will precede the Second Coming. Jesus comes back to town, high-fiving the raptured living and dead saints of God as he scoots past them in the air, and then ruling with them for a thousand years of righteousness on earth, geographically centered around the holy city of Jerusalem. The shiny, happy millennium is followed by the significantly less happy release of Satan from the Abyss. The devil assembles a mighty army to attack God's people. The evil forces gather for battle, "numberless as sand along the shore" (Rev. 20:8), only to be destroyed by fire from heaven in a handy dose of *deus ex machina*. Then comes the final judgment, which is either a really good or really bad experience, depending on your theological perspective.

There's one thing, however, that premillennialists can't agree on: the timing of the Rapture, a concept collected from something Paul wrote in 1 Thessalonians.[4] They're in agreement that the faithful will be lifted up to heaven when the trumpet sounds and Jesus

---

3. The influence of the Scofield Reference Bible can't be emphasized enough. It was huge in North America. During the 1950s, it was estimated that half of all conservative Evangelicals were using it, particularly in Bible schools, where it is said to have approached near-Scriptural status. Soon, believers were unaware of any distinction between the actual text of the Bible and Scofield's interpretation of it. Which is odd, considering Scofield is generally considered to have been a disreputable character who was regularly accused of fraud, embezzlement, corruption, and all-around unsavoriness.

4. 1 Thessalonians 4:16-17: "For the Lord himself will come down from heaven, with a loud command, with the voice of the archangel and with the trumpet call of God, and the dead in Christ will rise first. After that, we who are still alive and are left will be caught up together with them in the clouds to meet the Lord in the air. And so we will be with the Lord forever."

returns to gather up his Church. But they can't decide whether the Rapture is scheduled before, during, or after the Tribulation. Thus, you have three distinct flavors of premillennialism:

Pre-Tribulation Rapture ("pre-trib")—Because the Tribulation will be no fun at all, what with all the destruction and pain, believers catch major air before it all goes down. Which sounds great, but Jesus doesn't really seem to have gotten the memo about this plan when he details the end of the world in the Olivet Discourse (Matthew 24, Mark 13, Luke 21). Because he makes it pretty clear in this passage that the Rapture *follows* the Tribulation. Uh-oh. So pretribs ignore Jesus here and suggest that he'll actually return twice. Once before the Tribulation, to "secretly" take us all to heaven via the Rapture. Then he jets back to his Father's house to hang out for, oh, seven years or so. When things cool back down at the end of the Tribulation, he returns to earth again—this time in a highly visible, physical sense—to usher in his millennial reign. Nice.

Mid-Tribulation Rapture ("mid-trib")—The book of Daniel mentions a period of forty-two months after either the signing of a peace treaty or the halting of daily sacrifices in the Temple (don't ask), so mid-tribs argue the Rapture will open, to great applause, three-and-a-half years into the seven-year Tribulation. After which things get *really* bad. So Christians are still spared most of the hardship, but again you've got Jesus returning twice. And wouldn't he have known enough about his Second and Third Comings to mention both on the Mount of Olives?

Post-Tribulation Rapture ("post-trib")—In this system, the faithful have to go through the seven-year Tribulation along with all the heathens. Which is not fair at all. Critics of this belief get all huffy because the Bible says Christ's return can't be predicted.[5] They point out that everyone will presumably know when the Tribulation

---

5. The post-tribbers are dreamers. If there's one place premillennialists *don't* take the Bible literally, it's when it tells them in Matthew 24 that no one can predict Christ's return.

begins, what with the obvious ascension of the Antichrist and the kick-off of the peace season. Then forty-two months later, the whole thing takes a turn for the worse, hell-in-a-handbasket-style. Count out an additional forty-two months from that middle point, and you've got yourself the Rapture. Soooooo predictable. But then again, Jesus only comes back once according to this viewpoint, so at least you don't have to do any interpretive gymnastics when reading the red-letter parts of the Gospels.

Set aside the disputed sequencing of the Rapture, though, and you'll find that the various subdivisions of premillennialism have a bunch of beliefs in common. First, premills are really protective of the Jews as God's chosen people. This has everything to do with the theory of separate dispensations—God's relationship with the Christian Church is different from his continued relationship with those of Jewish ancestry and faith. Though most Jews don't believe Jesus to be their Messiah, God still looks after them and has a plan for them within the grand scheme of things. In fact, after the Tribulation, God will resume his long relationship with the Jews, fulfilling all those Old Testament promises about the restoration of the Temple, etc. So premills are usually major allies of the Jews and the State of Israel.

Secondly, premills can be aggressively evangelical in their attempts to win converts (or "decisions for Christ") based on a usually authentic desire to keep their friends, families, and coworkers from being "left behind" by the Rapture and subsequently exposed to the horrors of the Tribulation. Which you wouldn't wish on anyone. Even telemarketers.

Thirdly, premills are fanatical about prophecy. They interpret the Bible literally (well, *most* of the Bible) and remain on the lookout for fulfillments of those prophecies. A majority of your date-setters,

Antichrist-identifiers, and sign-watchers are probably dispensational premillennialists. They believe governments will increasingly grow evil as the Last Days approach. Wars will increase. Society will decay. The potato salad will go bad. Any peace will be fleeting and false. Premillennialists tend to take a negative view of the world around them, because the bad stuff—war, natural disaster, economic collapse, terrorism—is only a sign that The End is nearer than it used to be.

WHO BELIEVES THIS STUFF? Besides Darby and Scofield, you've got apocalyptic dignitaries like Hal Lindsey, author of *The Late, Great Planet Earth*; John Walvoord, author of *Armageddon, Oil, and the Middle East Crisis*; and Tim LaHaye, co-creator of the Left Behind series. Billy Graham and Jerry Falwell are also premill. Dallas Theological Seminary is virtually a mill of premillennialism. Most evangelical fundamentalists are onboard, too.

WHAT'S THE BEST PART ABOUT IT? No worries about the Tribulation (at least for the Pre-Tribs, who are the most common types of premills). And despite all the bad stuff happening, there's hope around the corner. Things will keep getting worse until they get so unbearably bad Jesus comes back. Wooo!

WHAT'S THE WORST PART? There's a teeny internal conflict within premillennialism. According to the theory, morality, sin, and hardship will increase up to the Lord's return. Yet, as dedicated Christians, premills feel the obligation to fight sinfulness and the decline of traditional values (typically, religious hot buttons like homosexuality, Hollywood immorality, abortion, and the like). But by fighting these things, are they actually prolonging the Rapture? Are they pushing back Christ's return? Some critics think so. But the Pocket Guide hardly figures that Jesus is pacing around up in heaven, frustrated because he keeps trying to come back, but can't, because his meddling followers keep making progress: "Wait! Hold the trumpets! The Republicans just got that obscenity law passed. Back to your clouds, everybody." Naw . . .

SYSTEM 3:
AMILLENNIALISM

The standard for most of the two thousand years of Christianity. Amillennialism is what Augustine proposed instead of historical (and heretical) premillennialism and its literal interpretation of Revelation.[6] Once amillennialism caught on, it was the formal belief of the Church up until Darby and Scofield started making waves, and some mainline Protestant denominations and many Catholics still adhere to it today.

So what is it? You'd think from the prefix that amillennialists don't believe in a millennial reign at all—despite what Revelation 20 says—but that's not precisely true. Instead, they don't believe in a *literal* one thousand-year reign following Christ's return. Amillennialists don't view the millennium in a future sense, as something that's gonna happen soon. They think it's already been realized—we're living in it now, during this period of time between the first coming (the first century manger-to-resurrection life of Christ) and the Second Coming. In fact, you'll occasionally see the belief referred to as "Realized Millennialism."

Amills reach this conviction by hypothesizing that the chapter-by-chapter breakdown of the book of Revelation is not necessarily chronological. So even though Jesus shows up for his return engagement in chapter 19, and the thousand years starts in chapter 20, no one says that has to be the exact order of events, right?

---

6. Back when the biblical canon was being set, many church fathers wanted to exclude Revelation from the list. Augustine argued that it should stay. But only if it was viewed as a symbolic account of the struggle between good and evil—not as a prophetic blueprint for the future.

Besides, in Revelation, the final judgment doesn't occur until after the thousand years. But Jesus says in Matthew 24 that it starts "when the Son of Man comes in his glory." So, they say, either Jesus has a wrong itinerary, or Revelation is out of sequence. And, "always side with Jesus" being a good rule of thumb, they choose the latter.

Accordingly, they believe the kingdom of God is something that's happening right here and now. Christ is reigning, with his Church, over the world, and we're right in the thick of it. We're already experiencing the Tribulation, too. We slog through a mix of good and bad until, finally, Jesus returns. Then comes the final judgment. Then the world and history as we know it are no more. Amillennialists consider most of the events detailed in Revelation and elsewhere in the Bible to be either symbolic in nature or describing something that's already happened. Same goes for the Antichrist. He's a symbolic figure, and not a real person. And Satan? Old news. Dude's already bound by Jesus' death on the cross, and therefore prohibited from any havoc-wreaking until his last gasp right before Christ's return.

Needless to say, many conservative Christians and biblical literalists are not too fond of amillennialism.

WHO BELIEVES THIS STUFF? Theological heavyweights like Origen, Augustine, and most of the Protestant Reformers, for one thing, since amillennialism has historically been a majority position within the Church. Members of the Lutheran Church-Missouri Synod and the Church of Christ are likely amillennialists, as are a good many Reformed and/or Catholic theologians (like J.I. Packer or William Hendrickson) whom you probably wouldn't recognize if they crawled up onto your shoulders and smacked you over the head with a bowl of wrath. Because it's not like amills are out writing action-packed "realized millennium" novels or anything.

WHAT'S THE BEST PART ABOUT IT? It's not literal, so no need for all the obnoxious date-setting and Rapture-predicting.

WHAT'S THE WORST PART? Actually, the date-setting and Rapture-predicting are sort of interesting. In a car-wreck kind of way.

SYSTEM 4:
POSTMILLENNIALISM

Everything's peachy, and gradually getting peachier. Postmillennialism came to prominence way back during the nineteenth century, peaking during the heady days of progress and technology from 1870 to 1915. Back then, folks were optimistic. World War I hadn't yet popped up, and American evangelicals were thriving after a period of religious revival and spiritual awakening.

Postmillennialism was custom-tailored to match this national confidence. Its adherents believe that the thousand years of peace and righteousness will happen *before* Christ's return to earth, which will then be followed by the final judgment. While postmills disagree on some of the details—whether or not it's a literal thousand years, whether or not it takes place in the future or is slowly materializing now—they all agree that Christians play a role in making sure it happens. Thanks to the hard work of believers and the grace of God, the world is gradually getting better. We're just a few steps shy of all-fixed, due to years and years of the influence of the Gospel. The world is slowly becoming Christianized, and at some point, the last person on earth—Osama bin Laden, perhaps? Or Michael Moore?—will respond to the Gospel. Which means a complete victory of the kingdom of God over unbelief. Satan will be subdued. Sin will be no more. We'll all strap on our "What Would Jesus Do?" bracelets and tumble right into God's golden age of peace, prosperity, and potluck every Wednesday night.

It's not all smiles and pats on the back, though, because at the end of the millennial reign, Satan gets released from hell and jogs on up to earth. That's when the period of great apostasy goes down, as described in Revelation 20. Forces of evil, battle of Armageddon, etc. But then Jesus shows up and kicks a little Beelzebutt. Later, after the judgment—which should be fairly quick, everyone on earth being so holy and everything—comes the resurrection of dead believers and the institution of the new heaven and new earth. Everyone grins.

Postmillennialism was huge at the turn of the last century, thanks to all the progress and good feelings about humanity's future. That is, until World War I came to town. It's hard to be optimistic about the fate of mankind when mankind is trying to, you know, kill each other with guns. It turned quite a few happy postmillennial smiles upside-down, and many began to question the veracity of the whole "yay, everybody's becoming a Christian" philosophy. In fact, many postmills got so depressed about society that they jumped right off the bus and bought a ticket for the Premillennialism Express, which was headed the opposite direction. And fast. Needless to say, postmills were few and far between during the middle part of the twentieth century.

But lately, there's been a resurgence in the theory, thanks to the always-interesting Pentecostal side of Christianity. They call it "Kingdom Now Theology" or "Dominion Theology," and its main thrust is that the charismatic revival—in the United States and especially in Third World countries—is God's way of reclaiming the earth from Satan and recapturing control over its government, culture, wealth, religion, and everything else. Once believers start to understand their role and potential for dominion under the guidance of the Holy Spirit (whom charismatics are really, really into), then they're on their way to establishing the kingdom of God on earth. Then, *boom!* Millennium.

The "dominion" part comes from Genesis 1:26, where God mentions that man will rule over "the fish of the sea and the birds of the air" and, well, everything else.

Another popular contemporary form of postmillennialism—separate from Dominion Theology—is called "Christian Reconstruction." It arose out of Presbyterianism in the 1970s and understands the job of the Church to be the gradual development of theocracy on earth and a return to biblical law based on the continuity of civil and moral law from the Old Testament to the New. Which is a mouthful, but basically means the Bible becomes the official law of the land. At that point, the Church can go about exercising its dominion over Satan and evil and bringing God's kingdom to earth. Needless to say, some people (atheists, liberals, pornographers) find Christian Reconstructionists to be a little scary.

WHO BELIEVES THIS STUFF? Remember Jonathan Edwards, the fiery New England Puritan preacher who many consider to be the greatest theologian in America's history? He was a postmillennialist. Old-time writers like A.A. Hodge and B.B. Warfield were well-known orthodox postmills (evidently, you had to have double initials to join the club), as is modern theologian R.C. Sproul, who also has some Preterist tendencies (keep reading). Current advocates of Dominion Theology are your illustrious Pentecostals and televangelists like Pat Robertson and Kenneth Copeland. And Christian Reconstructionists are represented by authors like Gary DeMarr and Gary North and the prolific R.J. Rushdoony of the Chalcedon Foundation.

WHAT'S THE BEST PART ABOUT IT? Because they're trying

to inaugurate the new age by making the world better—or at least holier—there's a lot of social activism among the postmillennialist crowd. You've got folks like Pat Robertson and the Christian Coalition attempting to bring the political process and societal morality back toward biblical norms. You've got friendly, reform-minded societies like those of the Puritans, who were genuinely interested in building a compassionate, close-knit community. And they gave us the Protestant work ethic, too. So that's good.

WHAT'S THE WORST PART? The whole theocratic bent makes people a little nervous, because if you sin or otherwise fall short of the glory of God, you're also breaking the law of the land. The results can be pretty harsh. After all, despite their contributions to early America, the Puritans were responsible for the wrongful imprisonments and unnecessary executions of the Salem Witch Trials.

And also? The Pocket Guide just isn't convinced things on earth are getting that much rosier.

SYSTEM 5:
PRETERISM

This one's easy. Preterists believe that all or most of the end-of-the-world events prophesied in the New Testament—the Tribulation, the rise of the Antichrist, the Second Coming, the battle of Armageddon—have already happened. Most of the book of Revelation, they believe, refers symbolically to the destruction of Jerusalem by invading Roman armies in and around 70 A.D.[7]

The big concerns for Preterists are the statements Jesus makes in the Gospel of Matthew regarding the Last Days. Stuff like Matthew 16:28, where he informs his disciples, "I tell you the truth, some who are standing here will not taste death before they see the

---

7. It helps that, in opposition to a lot of theologians who think it was written in the late first century, Preterists conveniently date the writing of Revelation in the late 60s A.D. Which was right about the time things started to heat up in Jerusalem.

Son of Man coming in his kingdom." Which typically leads to an exchange like this:

Skeptic to the Preterist: "Ha, ha, ha, dumb Christian. Jesus, your supposed Son of God, couldn't even get his prophecies right! You're worshiping a false prophet! How can you believe a word the Bible says?"

Preterist to the Skeptic: "Number one, shut up. Number two, the prophecies Jesus made were completely fulfilled in his followers' generation, because he was referring to the destruction of Jerusalem. So take that, you chicken-hearted pelican!"

Skeptic: "Chicken-hearted what?"

Preterist: "Shut up."

In order to preserve the inerrancy of the Bible and the accuracy of Christ's statements, full Preterists pay close attention to the events of the Roman-Jewish war, during which the Temple of Jerusalem burned to the ground. All the signs of the Last Days mentioned by Jesus on the Mount of Olives (Matthew 24) are in reference, they say, to this violent conflict—which many view as the divine judgment of God on Jerusalem via the nasty Romans. The Jewish historian Josephus describes the war like a first-century holocaust, with the entire city of Jerusalem engulfed by flame, heaps of bodies littering the ground, and blood flowing like water. No Jews were left alive—women, children, and the elderly all were put to the sword. Apocalyptic? Much.

Like most of these eschatological systems, Preterism is fairly complex. It divides itself into two camps. In camp number one, you have your hyper-Preterists (a.k.a. "full" Preterists), who believe that every single scriptural prophecy has been fulfilled—there's nothing else left on the calendar, including the resurrection of the dead and the Second Coming[8]—and that we are now living in the new heaven and new earth in our spiritually redeemed (and therefore resurrected) bodies. Seriously, we are. What, you didn't know?

Falling a little closer to the side of believability are the more conservative partial Preterists, who contend that *most* of the New Testament prophecies found fulfillment back in 70 A.D., but not *all*. They think the destruction of Jerusalem was *a* return of Christ, but not *the* return of Christ. It was *a* day of the Lord, but not *the* Day of the Lord. *A* judgment but not *the* final judgment.[9] It was the end of the Jewish Age, but not the end of history itself. Partial Preterists are still waiting for the Second Coming of Christ sometime in the future. Same goes for the resurrection of believers.

Typically, hyper-Preterists and partial Preterists don't like each other. The hypers think the partials are sellouts and not real Preterists at all. The partials think the hypers are on the edge of heresy. Sanity, too.

WHO BELIEVES THIS STUFF? A lot of folks who consider themselves postmillennialists or amillennialists hold to some of the tenets of partial Preterism, as many theologians throughout history—including influential early guys like Origen and John Chrysostom—have taught that at least some of Christ's prophecies found fulfillment in the days of Nero. Noted modern-day theologian R.C. Sproul is a well-respected postmillennialist who would identify himself as a partial Preterist, nicely explained in his 1998 book, *The Last Days According to Jesus*. And well-known "Bible Answer Man" radio host Hank Hanegraaff, along with Sigmund Brouwer, published a biblical prophecy novel in 2004 called *The Last Disciple*. It's sort of an anti-*Left Behind* (by no less than the same publisher), wrapping partial Preterist theology in the guise

---

8. The destruction of Jerusalem is seen as Christ's return to bring judgment upon the Jews, who rejected him a "generation" earlier.
9. Preterists are fond of italics.

of historical fiction set during the destruction of Jerusalem. (The Pocket Guide can only hope another dozen sequels are imminent.)

Full, hyper-Prets are few and far between, but their forefather was a guy named James Stuart Russell, who wrote a radical Preterist screed called *The Parousia* back in 1878. Modern adherents include Walt Hibbard and David Chilton. You haven't heard of them.

WHAT'S THE BEST PART ABOUT IT? It makes sense out of all the "this generation will not pass away" stuff Jesus says about the End of Days, which has always been problematic to believers and hot buttons for skeptics.

WHAT'S THE WORST PART? Those hyper-Preterists and their contention that we've been resurrected and are living spiritually in a new heaven and new earth are, to be honest, a little weird. Because what are all these terrorists and serial killers and maniacal despots doing here in Paradise? Shouldn't they be in the, um, smoking section?

BONUS SYSTEM: NON-MILLENNIALISM

This one's an extra because it's not so much a theological system as it is an anti-theology. Non-millennialists think all the interest in the prophecies of Revelation and the timelines and the various apocalyptic players is a load of hooey. Why? Because they see Revelation as nothing more than the nightmare of an old guy in exile. All that end-of-the-world stuff was just a freaky vision. The prophecies pretty much have nothing to offer us in terms of future events. If anything, Revelation was written to encourage early Christians to stand firm despite all the persecution by the Roman Empire. Because no matter how bad things get in Revelation—and let's face it, mass carnage turning rivers to blood is pretty bad—God still wins out in the end. Traditionally, liberal Christians and skeptics ascribe to this viewpoint. But conservative Christians are certain these guys are evil anyway, so who cares what they think? They're just missing out on all the Armageddon-pinpointing fun.

CHAPTER SIX

ARMAGEDDON GRAB-BAG
(MISCELLANEOUS ITEMS NOT LONG ENOUGH FOR CHAPTERS OF THEIR OWN)

- Interview with an End-Times Expert
- Six Potential End-of-the-World Scenarios (Courtesy of Nature)
- Six Potential End-of-the-World Scenarios (Courtesy of Science)
- The Endie Awards
- Further Reading

(INTERVIEW WITH PAUL MEIER)

INTERVIEW WITH AN END-TIMES EXPERT

Paul Meier has done a lot of things in his life. If by "a lot of things" you mean "a dizzying amount of achievement that would make robots look inefficient." At least it seems that way. He's a nationally recognized (and still practicing) psychiatrist, a pioneer in the field of integrating the physical nature of health with its psychological and spiritual dimensions. He's the founder and director of the well-respected Meier Clinics (there are twenty-two nationwide). He's the bestselling author, coauthor, or editor of more than seventy books, including *Happiness Is a Choice, Don't Let Jerks Get the Best of You*, the fictional End-Times thriller *The Third Millennium*, and its sequels. He has both a medical degree and a degree from Dallas Theological Seminary (the Mecca of premillennialist thought), where he taught for twelve years. He knows more Scripture than the pope. He travels the globe investigating biblical archeology. He can play anything on the piano if you'll hum a few bars. And he can juggle poisonous tree frogs with his feet.

Fine. That last one might be a stretch.

Paul Meier knows and does a lot of stuff, but one of his true passions is eschatology—the study of The End. So who better to talk to about biblical prophecy, the psychology of belief in the Rapture, and why he's not the world's most famous author of End-Times fiction?

It says right there in the title of this section that you're an expert on the End Times. In the interest of journalistic integrity, how about justifying that bold claim?

Well, I don't consider myself an expert on biblical prophecy, but I think I can make guesses as good as anybody else because of the following factors:

Number one, I have meditated on Scripture all my life. It was read to me every night at the supper table since I was born. I began reading and meditating on the Bible daily on my own when I was ten years old. I am almost sixty now and continue to do that daily, as I always have.

Two, prophecy has always been my favorite part of the Bible. I read books on it growing up. I took courses on it from the late Dr. John Walvoord [long-time president and chancellor emeritus at Dallas Theological Seminary and one of the world's leading scholars on Bible prophecy] while getting my seminary degree at DTS. I did a Bible prophecy tour of Israel with Babylon expert Charlie Dyer [another DTS professor and author of 1991's *The Rise of Babylon: Sign of the End Times*, about Saddam Hussein]. And I personally wrote four Bible prophecy novels.

Three, I memorized passages of Scripture from every single chapter in the Bible that had anything to do with prophecy, doing this up to four hours a day from 1985 to 1992.

And there are my professional credentials, of course. I'm a Christian psychiatrist of Jewish descent, although I did not find out both of my parents were part-Jewish until my mom finally let out the family secret in 1999, which is another story altogether. Anyway, I'm a psychiatrist who is very creative and right-brained (musical, intuitive, emotional, etc.), who has authored more than seventy books, who has a B.S. in Biology, an M.S. as an "Alumni

Distinguished Graduate Fellow" in Physiology, an M.D., a psychiatric residency from Duke University Medical School, and, of course, a seminary degree. And I'm the son of a third-grade-educated maid and a carpenter.

That's certainly impressive, but let's go back to number three. You memorized Scripture for four hours a day? For eight years?

Yes.

Are you kidding?

No.

Isn't that a little obsessive?

I am an obsessive person.

Please explain.

There are thirty-two thousand numbered deals of Microsoft's FreeCell game that come bundled with the Windows operating system on everyone's computer. I played FreeCell about three or four hours a day for several years until I conquered all of them, except number 11,982, which is impossible in my estimation.[1]

That's, um, interesting. Also a little disturbing.

So in 1985, I was the team doctor with a probe team that met up with astronaut Jim Irwin's team to climb Mt. Ararat because we thought that was the location of Noah's Ark, based on classified U.S. Air Force recon photos we had access to. But the Turks never let anyone go past the 16,500-foot level right above the Ahora Gorge. Irwin tried about five times, and the Turkish soldiers always

---

1. Author's note: He's right. According to Dave Ring's 1995 Internet FreeCell project, which tried to analyze the solvability of each Microsoft FreeCell deal, the only one that proved unsolvable by human or computer was 11,982.

accompanied these expeditions and always found reasons to divert us at the last minute. Once, Kurdish terrorists lined my team up in a firing squad and pretended like they were going to shoot, but then burned all our equipment instead and chased us down the mountain. Turkish soldiers rushed right up and found the terrorists and shot them dead on the spot.

Whoa.

Exactly. So I was very discouraged when I flew back to America empty-handed. Personally, I wanted the world to know the Ark was there. I wanted to help people believe the Bible, and I am sure the vain parts of myself wanted to be a member of the group who showed it to the world. That's when I felt like God was telling me to write a Bible prophecy novel instead, to wake people up to the truth of Scripture. I had a special burden for Jewish people even before I found out about my ancestry.

And like I said, I am an obsessive person. So after Ararat, I memorized prophecy verses for four hours a day from about 1985 to 1992. Not every day, really—but I probably averaged two to three hours a day. But I have meditated on Scripture and memorized verses for at least ten or twenty minutes a day ever since I was ten years old. And still do at 59, because I want to know everything and I want to keep growing more and more loving the older I get.

So after seven years of intense memorization, you put those verses to work and wrote the prophecy novel?

Yeah. After all the years of memorizing and after visiting Israel for details, street names, etc., I wrote *The Third Millennium*, my first Bible prophecy novel. I finished it in two weeks.

Two weeks!?!

My other three novels were written in one week each. They just flowed, like I was watching the typewriter to see what I had written. I can't claim divine inspiration, but it sure felt like he was helping me out since it flowed so easily, nonstop, with almost no corrections. *Left Behind*, by Tim LaHaye and Jerry Jenkins, came out a couple years later, though. And I think it is an excellent book. *Christianity Today* wrote an article comparing my novel to *Left Behind* and actually said mine was more biblical. The article seemed to imply they liked mine better, in a polite sort of way. But mine sold 300,000 and Tim's series sold 30 million.

Any ideas why? I mean, besides the fact that your book lacked a Kirk Cameron tie-in?

Maybe it was an act of God. Maybe it was the title. Maybe it was because mine told the whole Tribulation story all in one book and Tim's only told a little in each book, and people prefer that for some reason. Maybe Christians didn't like the fact that I rebelliously put the Rapture five years before the Second Coming of Christ, a time frame which no one—including myself—actually predicts. I just did it to show the world that no one knows whether the Rapture will happen immediately before the Second Coming, three-and-a-half years before, seven years before, or one hundred years before. Even Dr. Walvoord told me personally that no one knows. We only can guess.

I don't really know why *Left Behind* outsold mine, but I am very thankful that God blessed Tim LaHaye and his novel and used it to bring many people to Christ and to help lots of believers rededicate their lives to God. We're all on the same team. Tim is my teammate, and I pray for him and cheer him on. Only my vanity wishes it would have been mine that sold 30 million. The royalties would have been nice, too. But mostly the feeling of awe that must bring Tim, that he could help so many people.

You mentioned Dr. Walvoord, whom you studied under and taught with for several years at DTS. He was one of the most formidable prophecy scholars of the twentieth century. Yet even he admitted that a lot of this stuff is guesswork?

Here's a story. When Russia invaded Afghanistan in 1979, I was in the DTS faculty lounge, since I was teaching there full-time. Dr. Walvoord walked in and winked at me and said, "I sure hope we are right about this seven-year Rapture stuff." Now, according to Daniel 9:24-27, the Second Coming will occur seven years after the signing of some peace treaty between Israel and the Antichrist. So people jump to the conclusion that the Rapture will be the day of that signing or very close to it. But there really isn't any proof.

Regarding the invasion, Walvoord was implying that he hoped the war wasn't part of the Tribulation, since obviously we were there to witness it. We hadn't been raptured yet. Dr. Walvoord was brilliant, and probably the most knowledgeable Bible prophecy buff in the world when he was alive. But he was a lot more open-minded in his private conversations than he appeared in his writings, or in the things people accused him of.

And yet no one could even teach at Dallas Seminary unless he signed a doctrinal statement saying he believed the Rapture was seven years before the Second Coming. Go figure.

There's more to people's End-Times obsessions than just the religious aspect, right? From a psychological standpoint, it seems some people are hard-wired to get into that kind of thing more than others.

Some of my psychiatric patients hold their End-Times views based on their own wishful thinking, i.e., to escape from depression. Masochistic patients have excessive guilt, for instance, so they pick a religion that makes them think they'll go through the whole Tribulation period because they unconsciously want to relieve all their false guilt. Grace-oriented Christians want to believe they will escape all of it—the whole thing. And those in between want to believe they will suffer some of it, but escape the worst of it.

So it's possible to tell certain things about a person based on whether they are pre-trib, mid-trib, or post-trib regarding the Rapture?

Sure. It's often been said that most people on earth pick which sins they want to commit, then seek out a religion that will back them up. The same is true for prophecy. Some intellectual thinkers come to prophetic guesses based on logic and such, but certain personality types automatically congregate on certain viewpoints. Perfectionists—like some Dutch Reformed and Presbyterians, many of whom are better-educated and more financially well-off than most, but also more guilt-ridden—feel so insecure that they throw out Israel as rejected by God and put themselves in Israel's place as God's favorite child. Why? Maybe because, growing up, they felt more conditionally accepted by obsessive-compulsive parents who were totally difficult to please. So they take the whole Bible quite literally, like reading a newspaper, but they shift into a completely different gear when the Bible gets into anything prophetic. Then they go with a symbolic, vague interpretation of prophecy, like the Church began doing about three or four hundred years after Christ's death.

I think it's interesting that every generation seems to think theirs is the one in which Christ will return. No one seems to recall that every single generation has been saying that for two thousand years now, and every single one has been wrong. What makes us always think our generation is the lucky one?

I think all of us humans are a little narcissistic. We think the world revolves around us instead of the sun, so, of course, the Rapture has to be in our generation—why would God choose somebody else's? Plus, about half of the population of the world inherits a tendency to have dips in the serotonin levels in their brains. Serotonin is the primary chemical that gives us love, joy, peace, patience, and the other fruits of the Spirit. Anger can zap it, as can true or false guilt or unresolved grief or pot or alcohol or lack of sleep or too much stress. So people who are more depressed and even suicidal feel like killing themselves and think about it often, but won't actually do it for various reasons. So they pray intensely that either God will kill them or rapture them to ease their pain. I see patients like that several times a week in my psychiatric practice.

If I were God—and thank God I ain't—I would go ahead and let all the post-tribbers go through the tribulation, all the mid-tribbers go through half of it, all the pre-tribbers get raptured before any of the big mess. Then I'd let all the postmillennialists think they're God's favorite children and bypass the whole thing in some obscure part of the world where they could believe they were making the world better and better in preparation for the Lord's return.

I might even allow the schizophrenics to keep on thinking they were Jesus or the two prophets or Moses or Mary or whoever would make them feel a little relief from their extreme pain of insignificance. I once had three patients in one group therapy session who were all arguing with each other over which of the three was the real Jesus. One of them was a woman.

Did they settle the argument?

Yes, but I helped. I put all three on dopamine medicines, and by the next day or so, they all remembered who they really were, which was a big letdown for all three. Then I had to give them antidepressants.

So here's the big question. As a FreeCell-obsessed prophecy novelist and practicing psychiatrist, where do you stand personally on all this stuff? What are your beliefs regarding the Second Coming, the Rapture, etc.?

All my credentials and experiences and personal tendencies have combined to make me a very open-minded type of person who believes in the inerrancy of original Scripture, but who knows fewer and fewer dogmatic answers the older he gets. These things all prepare me to at least add some opinions on various prophetic views that are unique and outside the box. But I never claim to be right. I believe the Bible is always right, but purposely very vague, indirect, and often telescopic when it comes to prophecy ("telescopic" in the sense that, in some cases, one Old Testament prophecy may have multiple fulfillments in multiple centuries of the future). I believe God will clear things up when he is good and ready to, and he won't choose some arrogant TV evangelist begging for millions of dollars of donations to make the announcement. God resists the arrogant and gives grace to the humble.

So, to be honest, I am not an expert on Bible prophecy. I am an expert on the subject of why no one in his right mind, at this time, can be an expert on Bible prophecy.

(COURTESY OF NATURE)

SIX POTENTIAL END-OF-THE-WORLD SCENARIOS

We've been presuming, of course, that the world's demise will be God's doing. At some point, he'll decide to let loose the End of Days, paving the way for Armageddon and a showdown between good and evil. But who knows? Maybe the Almighty will let Creation do the dirty work for him. If so, he's got plenty of options. Here are six all-natural doomsday scenarios that, according to some scientists, could result in the end of the world as we know it:

❶ KILLER COMETS AND/OR ASTEROIDS

Around 65 million years ago, some sort of asteroid or comet nearly ten miles in diameter is thought to have slammed into earth off the coast of the Yucatan Peninsula. It left a 186-mile long hole. Mass extinction ensued, as 90 percent of species vanished. Bye-bye dinosaurs.

Circa 535 A.D., a dense swarm of space gravel swirled into our orbit, pummeling the atmosphere and kicking up enough debris to cause severely long winters. Crops died out. Nations were destroyed by famine, which might have been what plunged Europe into the Dark Ages.

Back in 1908, a comet fragment 130 feet wide flamed into Tunguska, Siberia. It exploded in the air, flattening a thousand square miles of uninhabited forest and detonating with a force estimated at ten megatons (700 times the power of the Hiroshima bomb). Had it hit a major metropolitan center like New York or Moscow, the city would have disappeared.

Could it happen again? Oh, yeah. Scientists say asteroids or comets with at least a six-mile diameter are big enough to cause global extinction by kick-starting a new Ice Age and showering the planet with corrosive rain. These killer space rocks bust through the door every 50 to 100 million years. Want scary? More than a thousand of these monsters are thought to exist in earth's general area, though none appear to be headed for us. At least not yet.

❷ SUPERVOLCANOES

Forget everything you know about Mount St. Helens or Pompeii. Those are molehills compared to the threat of supervolcanoes—which aren't right-there-in-plain-sight smoldering mountains, but huge, collapsed, underground craters called *calderas*. They're vast magma chambers loaded with molten rock and located miles beneath the surface. And when that subsurface pressure gets too intense for its surroundings? Boom.

A supervolcano called Toba erupted 74,000 years ago in Sumatra, pumping five billion tons of sulfuric acid into the atmosphere, along with enough rock, ash, and dust to reflect away all the sun's radiation. Another by-product? Tidal waves of molten lava. Post-Toba, the earth cooled as much as nine degrees Fahrenheit over the next several years. That's the difference between today and the last Ice Age.

Which active supervolcano is the next candidate for Tobasized tribulation? According to the U.S. Geologic Survey, it's none other than the Yellowstone caldera, a crater dozens of miles across and located directly beneath the famed National Park. Experts say it blows once every 600,000 years. Last eruption: some 640,000 years ago. Yeesh.

❸ SUPERMASSIVE BLACK HOLES

Just a few years ago, many scientists doubted black holes existed at all—until the Hubble Space Telescope turned far-out science fiction into fact. Not only do black holes the size of our solar system exist, but they're all over the place, dotting just about every galaxy the Hubble has peeked into.

Our personal apocalyptic black hole lurks in the heart of the Milky Way. It's three billion—yep, billion—times larger than our own sun, devouring space gas and random stars like a massive Pac-Man. It's the kind of thing that could destroy our whole solar system. How? Its massive gravitational influence starts to tug against the orbits of planets and their moons. Planetary wobbling ensues. Too much careening, and we get slingshot out of orbit. There go the nice temperatures. And distinct seasons. And, um, important things like the atmosphere. Get too far away from the sun, and we're Mars, frozen and uninhabitable. Get too close, and we roast.

And should one get near enough to actually slurp earth into its vortex? Then the gravity is so intense we just squish. Every atom gets crushed out of existence. Presently, we're so far away from our black hole that it's not much of a worry. But at least one physicist thinks the Milky Way will eventually collide with our neighboring galaxy, Andromeda. And when we do, the impact will surely send the whole solar system reeling, giving us a fifty/fifty chance at bumping into our black hole. Then we flat line. Of course, that's a good three billion years away, so don't break out the hardhats just yet.

❹ CLIMATIC SHIFTINESS

You thought gradual, one-degree-at-a-time global warming was bad? That's just a political issue. The real danger to our present society is a flip-flop. Not the shoe (which can be quite comfortable during all this global warming), but a climatic flip-flop—an abrupt shift in earth's temperature patterns. It can happen. A Denver scientist did some poking around into fossilized oxygen isotopes—or whatever—and figured out that, over the last 1.6 million years, our planet has experienced an abrupt temperature "flip" sixty-three times. That's an average of one every few thousand years.

We're currently living in a period of nice, temperate pleasantness. That's because the last big shift—out of the Ice Age and into the Backyard Barbecue Age—was ten thousand years ago. One flip every few thousand years . . . last flip ten millennia ago. Oooooh.

So what could happen? Well, all those greenhouse gasses we're building up with our factories and SUVs and flatulent livestock could trap so much heat in the atmosphere that our environment starts to break down. Polar ice caps could melt. Massive storms could develop. Oceanic currents might even see their courses altered. What if the warm Gulf Stream current, which is the primary reason January in Great Britain doesn't feel like January in Nova Scotia, suddenly turned tail on the cliffs of Dover? This is what would happen: Europe would go Popsicle even if the rest of the world was getting hotter.

And if all the warming continued, and Europeans started shivering, and everyone else started sweating, and crops started dying out, and icebergs started softening, and every nation of the world started thinking about hoarding and protecting their dwindling resources, then what? Then you have food, water, and energy becoming the most precious commodities around. And you have nations developing weapons of mass destruction in order to keep those resources safe. Which leads to global instability (even worse than right now). And terrorism (even worse than right now). And eventual Apocalypse because of all the anarchy. Maybe.

❺ MAGNETIC POLE-SWAPPING

Our planetary core is a big ball of liquid iron that's constantly in motion. That motion results in powerful electrical currents along its outside edge. And those currents are the primary reason earth has a magnetic field.

What's so cool about a magnetic field? Well, for one thing, it protects us from the harmful cosmic rays of the sun. Without it, we would all die—humans, animals, plants, even cockroaches—due to the heavy radiation. Plus, it's a great navigational aid, what with all the compass-needle-pointing-north stuff. Anyway, the magnetic field is important.

Recent geological research indicates that our magnetic field is gradually weakening by about 5 percent per century. Some researchers wonder if this might be the start of a magnetic pole reversal. The magnetic field slowly gets weaker and weaker until the north and south poles completely swap out. Such a reversal could be deadly. Huge, electrically charged bodies of lava would act like gigantic flowing magnets, abruptly repelling areas that once attracted them. The seismic movement would cause earthquakes, volcanoes, and tsunamis. Migrating birds would get all confused. Plant and animal life would disappear. We'd all get fried by cosmic radiation. And also: Your compass needle would start pointing to Antarctica.

The geological record indicates magnetic pole swaps have occurred in the past, apparently every 250,000 years or so. Last time it happened? Right around 750,000 years ago. Use your compasses now while they still work.

⑥ BURSTING GAMMA RAYS

Occasionally, the calm emptiness of the universe is disrupted by the sudden flash of high-energy photons. Scientists call these random and mysterious cosmic explosions gamma-ray bursts. They're big. Like, galaxy-big. Even larger than supernovas, which are the space-brightening death explosions of massive stars. Gamma-ray bursts last only a few seconds—sometimes even fractions of a second—but those seconds are unquestionably the most violent in the universe. No one knows what causes them. They explode and then disappear almost immediately, leaving no identifiable clue as to their source. Gamma-ray bursts are powerful, frequent, and hardly understood at all.

Until recently, scientists thought the nearest gamma-ray bursts were billions of light-years away from our little corner of the solar system. But then they discovered a cluster of them in a nearby galaxy, and have subsequently documented one hundred bursts less than 325 million light-years away. Which isn't quite too-close-for-comfort, but a lot closer than anyone thought. What would happen if one popped in our galaxy, perhaps only thousands of light-years away, firing its photons in our general direction?

Let's say one originates in the center of the Milky Way, which is thirty thousand light-years from our backyard. The results wouldn't be too bad—it would damage our ozone layer, but no more than a major volcanic eruption or a series of intense solar flares. But what if we get a burst three thousand light-years from earth? You guessed it—worldwide catastrophe. A burst of ten seconds or more would destroy our ozone layer for years, leaving us vulnerable to dangerous UV radiation. Which means skin cancer. And vegetation dying off. And acid rain. And ravaged ecosystems. And smoggy, darkened skies due to the sludgy combination of gamma rays with our atmospheric nitrogen. And therefore cooler temperatures worldwide. Long story short? Mass extinction.

Could a gamma-ray burst have been the death knell for the dinosaurs? Some scientists admit it's a possibility. Chances are we'll never have to face the effects of one in our neck of the celestial woods. But then again, you never know.

(COURTESY OF SCIENCE)

SIX POTENTIAL END-OF-THE-WORLD SCENARIOS

Nature's not the only candidate for worldwide destruction. Science and technology could also be culprits for cataclysm, particularly since our ongoing advances in these two interrelated fields are busting out more rapidly—and unpredictably—than ever before. Could a traditionally good thing like scientific progress bring about the demise of civilization? It's not out of the question. Here's how:

❶ HIGH-ENERGY PHYSICS

Back in 2000, after ten years of round-the-clock construction, the legendary Brookhaven National Laboratory in Long Island, New York, declared its Relativistic Heavy Ion Collider (RHIC) open for business. First item on the agenda was atom smashing—banging subatomic particles together just to see what would happen. At BNL, a circular magnet-driven contraption more than two miles long accelerates beams of gold ions to the speed of light and then—like a kid with a Hot Wheels® car in each hand—plows them into each other. The scientists watch with glee, then check out the atomic wreckage. The goal of these experiments is to create a quark-gluon plasma, a building block of matter they think might have been around at the time of the universe's Big Bang. (But which might actually be an exotic-sounding pseudo-scientific nonsense phrase they made up as an excuse to smash stuff. We're checking on it.)

To get to the quark-gluon plasma stage, though, you run a certain risk. Each of those collisions releases a teensy bit of energy that's ten thousand times hotter than the sun. Good thing these collisions are really, really small. But what if the particle-pile-ups accidentally create something else—like a runaway "strangelet"? Strangelets are subatomic particles that, unfortunately, aren't too well understood. What we do know is that they devour matter. Which we're made of. Uh-oh. Because if a negatively charged strangelet happens to be created during a smash-up, It could potentially set off a chain reaction that literally consumes everything in its path. The process is pretty simple: the created strangelet strips away the electrons of normal atoms and absorbs the exposed nucleus. The atom with the naked nucleus turns into a strangelet. Then the next one goes strangelet, too. And then the next one. The relentless process of expanding nothingness continues until we're all strangelets. Everyone. Everything. As in, bye-bye, universe as we know it.

Just a popular theory. The Brookhaven scientists say there's nothing to worry about. Are you reassured?

❷ OUT-OF-CONTROL NANOBOTS

Jurassic Park author Michael Crichton tapped into this fear with his 2002 thriller *Prey*, which features a last-ditch effort by scientists to destroy a swarm of self-replicating nanobots poised to take over the world. What? Nanobots?

Yep. So far they're theoretical, but according to people who actually know what they're talking about (as opposed to, for instance, the Pocket Guide), the existence of nanobots isn't so much a matter of "if" but "when." As in, they're coming.

First, a primer: Nanotechnology is the science of manipulating matter at the atomic level—building stuff from the molecule-up for the purpose of accomplishing certain goals. Wrinkle-free khakis? That's the mundane version of nanotech. But check out the stuff on the drawing board. How about military exoskeletons that allow soldiers to jump twenty feet in the air and repel bullets? Or photovoltaic molecular technologies that can turn a houseplant into a solar-powered generator? Or DNA-fueled motors that drive microscopic machines, smaller than red blood cells, which can be injected into our bodies for the purpose of seeking out and destroying cancers or viruses? Very cool. That's why geeks get excited about nanotechnology.

It's also why doomsayers get nervous about it. Because nanotech is so small, it must depend on self-replicating (and self-assembling) nanobots—the microscopic machines above—to generate enough force or activity to make stuff work. But what if something unexpected happens? Perhaps a software failure? A teensy-weensy short-circuit? What if these hypothetical nanobots go haywire on the self-replication, pilfering atoms from the surrounding environment, breaking their neighborhoods down, and reassembling all available molecules into clones of themselves? Before long, the earth will have been devoured by micro machines, and all that's left is a gunky slush—what K. Eric Drexler, the father of nanotechnology, once described as "gray goo."

And it all starts with wrinkle-free khakis. Be afraid.

❸ SUPERPLAGUE

Weaponized anthrax and smallpox are at the top of the list of societal worries these days. We're concerned that terrorists could get their hands on deadly bio-agents and let loose an epidemic in one of our cities. But of greater concern is a genetically modified superbug.

In 2003, a research team at St. Louis University, backed by a federal grant, engineered a form of mousepox virus designed to evade vaccines. They spliced a gene known to suppress the immune system into the mousepox virus, then injected the resulting combo into mice who had already been vaccinated against mousepox. The vaccinated mice died.

And a few years ago, government geneticists inserted genes from *E. coli* bacteria into *Deinococcus radiodurans*, an organism that—along with cockroaches and the Three Stooges—can survive an atomic blast. The result is a recombinant superbug with the ability to digest the toxic mercury leftovers at nuclear weapons production sites. They intend to someday release the bioengineered bacteria into the soil and groundwater at these sites to reduce pollution.

Should we lose sleep over super-mousepox or nuke-eating bacteria? Not exactly. But some fear that our genetic tinkering with naturally occurring viruses and bacteria could lead to the creation of a superplague—a bioengineered microbe that bypasses the immune system, or perhaps a killer virus that resists our efforts to vaccinate against it. At any rate, we end up with a disease that's worse than anything we've ever seen. And with the way biotechnology is spreading—which, to be honest, is a lot faster than most bioethicists are comfortable with—it's not too far-fetched to envision a future where regular people can concoct super-diseases as easily as a kid stinking up his basement with a chemistry set.

❹ GENETICALLY ENHANCED CLASS WARFARE

What if we use our newfound knowledge of the human genome to genetically enhance our offspring? It might be possible someday, but it would also be very expensive. Those who can afford it could start tweaking their kids' genetic codes to make them smarter and prettier and more athletic and even healthier. But the non-wealthy of the world? The poor people? Money's tight, so no genetic enhancement for little Junior.

He'll just have to make it on his own.

Doomsday theorists are spooked by the potential: two distinct classes of humanity. A rich, strong, intelligent upper class—those who could afford to be engineered to perfection—and a "subhuman" servant class made up of those who couldn't. A nice little twist on the "haves" and the "have-nots," with the have-nots becoming a less-important offshoot of the human species. Evolutionary biologists say such a split could lead to the end of the race altogether. How? The enhanced superhumans get annoyed at the inferior underclass, and decide to destroy them. The underclass despises the Richie Riches with their high IQs and ability to tear phone books in half (which is what the Pocket Guide would do with super-strength) and decides to destroy them. Aaaaaand cue the apocalyptic class warfare.

Could it happen? Surely not, what with humanity's stellar record when it comes to ugly issues like racism and genocide. (Snerk.)

❺ ARTIFICIAL INTELLIGENCE

Stephen Hawking is, like, the smartest guy in the world. He's a world-famous physicist, focusing on theoretical cosmology and quantum gravity, whatever that means. He's a full-fledged genius and the bestselling author of *A Brief History of Time*. He's the Lucasian professor of mathematics at Cambridge—a post once held by Sir Isaac Newton, for crying out loud. So when he makes a "better watch out" kind of statement, well, we'd better watch out.

Stephen Hawking thinks mankind will eventually be overrun by computers, according to a 2001 interview he gave with the German newsmagazine, *Focus*. Unlike human intellect, he said, computers double their intelligence every eighteen months or so. Which means they could eventually create their own independent brainpower, making themselves "smarter" than us, similar to our being "smarter" than animals. And then? Then the machines take over the world. In terms of apocalyptic scenarios, it's very similar to *The Matrix*, but with less kung fu.

But don't worry, Hawking told his interviewers. All we have to do to prevent this from happening is to improve our own intelligence through genetic engineering. Wait a second—improve our own what? He didn't just say "genetic engineering," did he? What, did he skip over scenario number four?

Some genius.

❻ NUCLEAR ARMAGEDDON

If you thought we were past this, think again. So far, everything's pretty cool between the superpowers. The United States is chugging along, business as usual, saving the world left and right. China has been behaving itself. Russia doesn't do much of anything anymore besides export vodka and disgruntled scientists. But how long will the *kumbaya*-singing last? And what about the newly nukified Pakistan and India? North Korea probably has nuclear capabilities, too—held in check by no less than Kim Jong-il, a clinically insane, sex-crazed alcoholic dictator. And if North Korea has the bomb, can Japan be far behind? South Korea? Iran? New Jersey?

If there's any potential doomsday scenario that we can't mark off the list, it's worldwide nuclear catastrophe. Back during the Cold War, the United States and U.S.S.R. had enough intercontinental ballistic missiles (ICBMs) to destroy each other several times over. Thankfully, we're past the nail-biting days of mutually assured destruction, but nuclear annihilation isn't off the table. There are still plenty of warheads out there, and just enough ideologues with itchy trigger fingers to cause problems. Should some sort of large-scale nuclear deployment develop—especially over highly flammable targets like cities—we would likely be in for a hypothetical nuclear winter. The smoke and soot would clog up the stratosphere and black out sunlight for weeks or years. Temps would drop dramatically. Killing frosts. Nuclear fallout. No food. Destroyed ozone and radiation risk. Shattered infrastructure—the transportation, medical, and economic systems would be in chaos. People would be dying all over the place.

And you're worried about runaway nanobots? Yikes.

(RECOGNIZING EXCELLENCE IN APOCALYPTIC ENTERTAINMENT)
THE ENDIE AWARDS

The last decade has been like a *Perfect Storm* for end-of-the-world entertainment, as several independent factors converged to give an apocalyptic boost to the industry. The year 2000 approached and then passed us by. Tensions continued to grow in the Middle East. Global terrorism spiked, hitting home on September 11, 2001. And the novels of the Left Behind series became overnight bestsellers, convincing the secular world that End-Times entertainment could become a major growth industry.

Of course, Christians already knew this. Which is why there are tons of movies, books, and even television programs with plots wrapped around the drama inspired by Revelation. There's no way you'll ever get around to watching all these movies or reading all these books—in fact, the Pocket Guide recommends against it, since many of them are nail-gun-to-the-head torture.

But that shouldn't keep us from celebrating this tidy little pocket industry. Following are the first annual Endie Awards, recognizing the best (and worst) in End-Times entertainment.

LIFETIME ACHIEVEMENT AWARD

Paul and Peter Lalonde. The Canadian-born Lalonde brothers of Cloud Ten Pictures are admired throughout the film industry—and that's the whole film industry, not just the apocalyptic one—for having developed one of the most successful independent film studios in the English-speaking world. The primary demographic for their films? Christians on the lookout for chaste thrillers with high production values. Which means the Rapture and the Tribulation are central plot devices. Cloud Ten scored its breakout hit with *Left Behind: The Movie* in 2000, based on the first novel in the series. It was the number-one-selling video during its first week of release and went on to sell 3 million copies. It was followed by *Left Behind II: Tribulation Force*. The Lalondes are also the producers of several other successful straight-to-video Christian pics starring washed up Hollywood veterans, including 1997's *Apocalypse*, and its sequels *Revelation* (with Jeff Fahey), *Tribulation* (with Gary Busey and Margot Kidder), and *Judgment* (with Corbin Bernsen).

BEST STUDIO PICTURE

Armageddon (1998). A monster asteroid is hurtling toward earth, and the geniuses at NASA, despite millions of dollars of funding, are only able to come up with one option—to recruit Bruce Willis and his rag-tag team of deep-core drillers to help astronauts learn how to dig into the rock and nuke it to pieces. But Bruce Willis being a major star and everything, it appears there's an even better option: turn the drillers themselves into astronauts! That makes sense. So Bruce and company become spacemen after only a few days of training. They tie up some personal loose ends, blast into space, enjoy some goofy male bonding, land on the asteroid, drill a big hole, and blow the thing up. Meanwhile, the citizens of earth prepare for The End. (Directed by Michael Bay. Also starring Ben Affleck, Owen Wilson, Billy Bob Thornton, and Liv Tyler.)

HONORABLE MENTION: *The Day After Tomorrow* (2004).

BEST INDEPENDENT FILM

Apocalypse III: Tribulation (2000). A Cloud Ten Pictures production, in which Gary Busey stars as a police detective and all-around good guy who discovers his family is the target of a dark conspiracy, possibly satanic in origin. Then he gets hit by a truck. When he wakes up from a coma, he makes another frightening discovery: The world is being ruled by a self-appointed Messiah! And everyone is wearing "666" marks on their right hands! And the same dark forces from before the accident are still hunting him! Good thing he hooks up with an underground gaggle of resistors, out to expose the so-called Messiah as the Antichrist. (Directed by André Van Heerden. Also starring Howie Mandel, Nick Mancuso, and Margot Kidder. No, really!)

HONORABLE MENTION: *Left Behind: The Movie* (2000)

BEST CLASSIC RAPTURE MOVIE

A Thief in the Night, the super low-budget, scare-the-people-into-salvation film that kicked off the church basement Rapture film industry in 1972. In it, we meet hip, young Iowans before the Rapture and then watch them flee from the red-and-orange striped vans of the one-world government that crops up afterward. *A Thief in the Night* was one of the most successful films in the history of religious media and spawned three sequels.

BEST NOVEL

Left Behind: A Novel of the Earth's Last Days, by Tim LaHaye and Jerry Jenkins. The 1995 book that started the *New York Times*-bestselling phenomenon, *Left Behind* begins aboard a commercial airliner that suddenly experiences a minor in-flight problem, as a bunch of its passengers disappear into thin air! Turns out it was the Rapture, and a slick international politician named Nicolae Carpathia takes control of the UN to restore order and, well, set up a one-world government. And while he's at it, a one-world religion, too. Which revolves around him. (He gets named *People* magazine's "Sexiest Man Alive," though, so no one bats an eyelash.) Meanwhile, a bunch of those "left behind" get religion, identify Carpathia as the Antichrist, and start calling themselves Tribulation Force. They go to work opposing the New World Order and such. The books of the Left Behind series are juicy, slapdash thrillers wrapped around traditional premillennialist theology. They were thought to culminate in the 2004 release of the twelfth book in the series, *Glorious Appearing*. Until it was announced that there would be three "Countdown to the Rapture" titles—prequels—released in 2005-2006. And then book sixteen, about the final judgment, shows up in 2007.

HONORABLE MENTION: The Third Millennium, by Paul D. Meier (1993). Read an interview with Paul Meier on page 130.

BEST USE OF WIDE MARGINS AND OVERLY LARGE TYPE TO EXTEND A PROFITABLE FRANCHISE

Books two through twelve of the Left Behind series, which was originally conceived as a trilogy. The Pocket Guide presumes upcoming books will also follow this pattern.

BEST TELEVISION PROGRAM

Buffy the Vampire Slayer. Not all apocalyptic programming has to involve the Rapture, you know. Back in the series' hey-day, Buffy Summers (Sarah Michelle Gellar) and her Scooby gang faced down evil once a week in the form of vampires, killer robots, the occasional rogue demon, and, every so often, an ancient and powerful evil bent on world destruction. It's the world-destruction part that earns Buffy its own Endie—every season seemed to end with the Slayer turning the tide on a potential worldwide apocalypse. When Buffy died after averting yet another end-of-the-world scenario at the end of Season Five (she would eventually be resurrected), her tombstone read, "She saved the world a lot." Good job, Buffy.

HONORABLE MENTION: Millennium, created by Chris Carter and starring Lance Henriksen as a criminal profiler on the trail of a huge governmental conspiracy that may or may not have something to do with the end of the world. Chris Carter was the apocalyptic mind behind *The X-Files*, which also deserves a shout-out.

BEST PORTRAYAL OF SATAN

Satan, as voiced by Trey Parker, in the animated *South Park: Bigger, Longer, and Uncut.* Poor little Kenny dies, goes to hell, and finds out Satan is carrying on an affair with the newly arrived Saddam Hussein. Turns out Saddam's in it for the lovin', while the devil really wants to connect on an emotional level. They get counseling.

NEXT BEST PORTRAYAL OF SATAN

Al Pacino's gleeful, scenery-chewing turn as the boss of a diabolical law firm in *Devil's Advocate*. The 1997 film also starred Keanu Reeves and Charlize Theron.

BEST USE OF AN INTIMIDATING BLACK MAN

Cloud Ten's *Judgment* (2001), starring Mr. T as a man of action who's tired of all the namby-pamby Christians' passive resistance against the Antichrist. He says stuff like: "They want fire and brimstone, they're gonna get it!" It's pretty much a Christian version of T's A-Team character, B.A. Baracus. Which is cool.

WORST USE OF AN INTIMIDATING BLACK MAN

Cloud Ten's *Deceived* (2002), starring Louis Gossett, Jr., as a power-mad general who tries to gain control of a remote space observatory after it receives a signal thought to be extraterrestrial in origin. Turns out the ET signal is some sort of mind-controlling tool of Satan. Or whatever. For the most part, Gossett just frowns a lot and looks mean.

BEST USE OF GARY BUSEY

Tribulation (2000), in which Busey's character gets hit by a truck and falls into a coma after stumbling onto a psychic conspiracy, waking up to a frightening world ruled by the Antichrist. Back in 1988, the real-life Gary Busey had a bad motorcycle accident and was unconscious for months with a major head injury. He woke up to a world in which he was a has-been actor with frighteningly large teeth.

BEST USE OF A FORMER TEEN HEARTTHROB

Left Behind: The Movie (2000) and its sequel, starring Kirk Cameron—the wisecracking Mike Seaver from television's *Growing Pains*—as Buck Williams, a hotshot television reporter who tries to figure out what's going on amid the chaos following the Rapture.

HONORABLE MENTION: Judd Nelson in *Deceived*.

ONLY USE OF A FORMER TEEN HEARTTHROB NAMED KIRK CAMERON

Left Behind: The Movie and its sequel, because what else has Kirk Cameron been doing lately?

WORST USE OF A FORMER SUPERMODEL

Former *Sports Illustrated* Swimsuit Issue cover girl Carol Alt in Cloud Ten's *Revelation* (1999). She plays a beautiful blind cynic who, as a Christian member of the underground Antichrist resistance, fails to appear in any sort of swimwear at all.

BEST ARGUMENT AGAINST BABY-SWAPPING

The Omen (1976), in which Lee Remick—married to wealthy politician Gregory Peck—loses consciousness while delivering a stillborn baby. The resourceful Peck manages to "adopt" an infant whose mother died during a childbirth that occurred at the exact same time, replacing his dead child with the new one before his wife wakes up. And no one's the wiser, until little Damien turns out to be the Antichrist, and everyone around him suffers a grisly death. Should've known.

FURTHER READING

The following books were invaluable resources in the writing of this book. And they're gobs more scholarly than the Pocket Guide, if that's what you're into:

Richard Abanes, *End-Time Visions: The Doomsday Obsession* (Broadman & Holman, Nashville: 1998).

Stephen Jay Gould, *Questioning the Millennium: A Rationalist's Guide to a Precisely Arbitrary Countdown* (Harmony Books, New York: 1997).

Alex Heard, *Apocalypse Pretty Soon: Travels in End-Time America* (Main Street/Doubleday, New York: 1999).

Richard Kyle, *The Last Days Are Here Again: A History of the End Times* (Baker Books, Grand Rapids, Michigan: 1998).

Tom McIver, *The End of the World: An Annotated Bibliography* (McFarland & Company, Jefferson, North Carolina: 1999).

James Randi, *The Mask of Nostradamus: The Prophecies of the World's Most Famous Seer* (Prometheus Books, Amherst, New York: 1993).

Thomas Robbins and Susan J. Palmer, *Millennium, Messiahs and Mayhem: Contemporary Apocalyptic Movements* (Routledge, New York: 1997).

Eugen Weber, *Apocalypses: Prophecies, Cults, and Millennial Beliefs through the Ages* (Harvard University Press, Cambridge, Massachusetts: 2000).

Daniel Wojcik, *The End of the World As We Know It: Faith, Fatalism, and Apocalypse in America* (New York University Press, New York: 1997).

These websites were also helpful:
A Brief History of the Apocalypse (*www.abhota.info*)

The Millennium and End-of-the-World Prophecies (*www.religioustolerance.org/end_wrld.htm*)

Frontline: Apocalypse!
(*www.pbs.org/wgbh/pages/frontline/shows/apocalypse*)

It's the End of the World as We Know It . . . Again!
(*www.geocities.com/Athens/Oracle/9941/index.html*)

This website was not helpful in the least:
Balloonhat (*www.balloonhat.com*)

The End-of-the-World Scenarios (Courtesy of Nature and Science) in this chapter were inspired by the skeptical fun of Gregg Easterbrook's "We're All Gonna Die!" from the July 2003 issue of *Wired*.

And, because he's a nice guy who graciously withstood the stupid questions of the Pocket Guide, you should read one of the great Dr. Paul Meier's many dozens of books. Start with *The Third Millennium* (Thomas Nelson, Nashville, 1993), even though it's a little cheeseball. At least it's shorter than the Left Behind series.

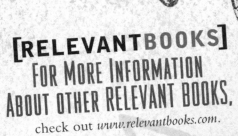